Into the Maze:

An Introduction to Intelligent Tools in HRTechnology

By John Sumser

An HRExaminer Industry Analysis

Table of Contents

EXECUTIVE SUMMARY — 3

INTRODUCTION — 6
    FOCUS & INITIATIVE — 9
    RAW FUNCTIONALITY — 10

DEFINING THE TERRAIN — 12
    OVERVIEW — 12
    THE TECHNOLOGY — 13

MARKET MAP — 19

ETHICAL CONSIDERATIONS — 28

LATENCY — 35

TOTAL COST OF OWNERSHIP (TCO) — 39

21 COMMON USE CASES — 46

FORECASTS — 48

COMPANIES WE DIDN'T COVER THIS TIME — 51

APPENDIX: COMPANY PAGES — 53

ACKNOWLEDGMENTS — 111

ABOUT — 112

Executive Summary

The levels of hype, hope, anxiety and dread surrounding Artificial Intelligence are intense. The buzz is in popular culture and in our offices. Fears of replacement by robots are coupled with dreams of the end of drudgery. Cars that drive themselves transport workers to resorts in a paradise where there is no more work. Starving hordes rail against the fortresses of wealth unable to afford today's ration of Soylent Green.

This report attempts to bring some common sense to the parts of the discussion that directly affect Human Resources Departments and their technology.

Although the story is more complex than this, 90% of the companies covered in the report offer a service directly related to Recruiting. Recruiting is where technology usually takes root in HR. It's the place where 'land and expand' strategies land.

The second part of this report contains detailed reviews of 30 companies, their offerings and business models.

Here are the highlights.

- We began the report as an investigation into Artificial Intelligence. We were unable to find actual AI. That doesn't mean that the work is not important. It means that calling it AI distracts from the value that these companies are creating.

- We considered describing the tools 'machine led decision making' because the services (save one) all deliver recommendations and guidance. There is a fair chance that those recommendations will be implemented without much consideration. Who can argue with a machine? And how would you do it?

- We settled on the idea of intelligent software. It captures the basic ethic of all the vendors: software should deliver more value with less time spent in the interface.

- We spoke with academics from all the major AI centers in North America. A conversational consciousness with the ability to innovate on the fly in conversation is a clear and shared definition of Artificial Intelligence. There is none in HRTech or anywhere else. Yet.

- Intelligent software involves tools that begin with pattern recognition and learn as those patterns change.

- The number of vendors offering intelligent software tools will grow to include all vendors of HRTechnology. This is really a fundamental set of technical capabilities.

- The reviewed vendors deliver 21 discrete use cases (usage scenarios). While some companies address the same issues or tasks, it is rare that two companies solve the same problem the same way. There are 89 total variations on the use cases. Unlike traditional software, each purchasing decision involves buying that vendor's opinion on the best way to solve a specific business problem.

- It is a nascent market. Huge benefit will accrue to companies that are willing to be early customers. But, the windfalls are accompanied by significant risks.

Latency is the lag between a change in reality and the machine's capacity to represent it. It is the most challenging question in the technical management of intelligent software.

- There are a host of ethical questions. We offer a chapter about some of them.

- Few vendors can adequately articulate the total cost of ownership of intelligent software. We provide an initial map to understand what is truly involved.

Here are the five questions you should use to begin a conversation with a vendor.

1. How long does it take the machine to learn something new? Can you define that both in calendar time and the number of transactions?

2. What are the feedback loops we should use to monitor the tool's alignment with our culture, processes, and procedures?

3. What is the process by which we inform the device that it is missing something or needs to learn something new?

4. If the machine makes a recommendation and we think it's out of date, what do we do?

5. What sort of staff do we need to ensure the performance of our intelligent software?

Introduction

This report covers the emergence of a new kind of software as represented by 30 companies. These vendors range from small operations, who are pre-investment, to the biggest players in HR Technology. Originally, the idea was to investigate and illuminate Artificial Intelligence in HRTech.

What we found was an enormous pile of unsubstantiated hype. If we were being kind, we'd describe the situation as 'aspirational labeling' or possibly 'overreaching by marketing.' Harsher language isn't particularly useful. Suffice it to say, there was no Artificial Intelligence to be found.

In the process of doing the research, we visited with experts in AI from Stanford, Berkeley, MIT, Harvard, and the University of Toronto. When we asked these experts what AI was, they painted a picture of a conversational consciousness. In that conversation, the intelligent machine would be able to innovate on the topic and interpret/respond to nuance and inference.

The academics have a pretty consistent definition of AI.

There is nothing like that happening in the halls of HR Technology. The most advanced tools are extremely mechanistic and limited when compared to a dynamic conversational intelligence. Companies that lay a strong claim to having AI functions look silly for the most part (although there are a few exceptions).

What we found instead was an amazing wonderland of experimentation. The companies we cover in this report are all charting unique paths through technology in pursuit of demonstrable value. It's a new flavor of Research and Development.

In the 20th century, R&D Laboratories were huge monolithic environments with extensive teams of really smart people. The conventional wisdom was that if you handled the environment well enough, someone would produce something interesting. It was a model pioneered by Thomas Edison, perfected by the telephone companies, and still has remnants in companies like Intel, Apple, HP, Cisco and other tech giants.

That approach doesn't really work in an environment of industrial disruption. We learned early in the digital era that the pioneers of bulk R&D failed because they couldn't get out of their own way. Polaroid failed to thrive, disc makers went under, music dematerialized. Investors began to distrust large scale technical innovation initiatives.

The result is a generation of technical companies that resemble single functions on a dropdown menu more than whole companies. The new model is that software companies are not only responsible for R&D, they have to prove its value in the market. Having a good idea is not enough. Investors are more interested in good ideas that make money.

Each of the thirty companies are engaged in a deep exploration (some likelier to succeed than others) of a slice of the HR continuum. Their approaches and differentiation are covered in detail in individual two page write-ups that is the second half of this report. It is worth noticing that the 30 companies we reviewed represent 30 different (and usually compelling) initiatives. Even when they are focused on the exact same problem and solution, they are profoundly different.

When a new technology emerges, the early adopters are rewarded disproportionately for investing early. At the same time, there is an enormous range of career risks associated with backing the wrong horse.

The goal of this report is to bring some coherence to understanding what is out there, what is coming, and how to think about where and when to make an investment.

These are the very early days of a very different way of interacting with software. It's not Artificial Intelligence, but it is very different from the software we are used to. There are new ethical issues, new technologies, and new approaches to intractable problems. This is the first edition of an annual research project that will attempt to keep you up to speed as the movement progresses.

The following tables describe the vendors we cover in this report and their functionality from a traditional perspective. It's a useful point of departure, but it hardly tells the whole story. The first table describes the primary focus, and gives a nutshell summary of the initiative. The second table highlights raw functionality. (There is an additional table in the use cases chapter that illuminates the interesting overlaps between these players.)

FOCUS & INITIATIVE

COMPANY	WEBSITE	FOCUS	MACHINE LED DECISION MAKING FUNCTIONALITY
Bradio	braidio.com	L&D	Accelerates learning in large, high volume call centers.
Burning Glass	burning-glass.com	WORKFORCE PLANNING	Deconstructs jobs into skills for strategic plans that work. Labor market trend analysis.
Ceridian	ceridian.com	SPECTRUM	Flight Risk Assessment based on time keeping data, embedded client performance.
Cornerstone on Demand	cornerstoneondemand.com	SPECTRUM	Full platform strategy with learning acceleration as the starting point.
Crowded	crowded.com	RECRUITING	Candidate database refresh using intelligent data market.
Engage Talent	engagetalent.com	RECRUITING	Predicts the likelihood that a prospective candidate will be receptive to an offer.
Glint	glintinc.com	ENGAGEMENT	Real time employee surveys with predictive capacity.
HireMya	hiremya.com	BOT (RECRUITING)	Bot/recruiting automation.
Hiretual	hiretual.com	RECRUITING	Sourcing with a virtual assistant. Contact gathering. Task automation.
HireVue	hirevue.com	RECRUITING	Video Interviewing plus facial recognition based assessment and performance prediction.
Humanyze	humanyze.com	NETWORK BEHAVIOR	Physical and digital measurement of the company as a network.
IBM	ibm.com	RECRUITING	Watson goes to the recruiting department.
Joberate	joberate.com	RECRUITING	Measures and predicts employee job changing behavior.
Joyous	joyoushq.com	COMMUNICATIONS	Engagement assessment from a continuous flow of employee communications.
karen.ai	karen.ai	BOT (RECRUITING)	Assesses candidates by matching team personality and culture fit.
Koru	joinkoru.com	RECRUITING/SELECTION	Predictive hiring for fit.
Kronos	kronos.com	SPECTRUM	Audits and highlights anomalies in time and attendance record keeping.
Leap.ai	leap.ai	RECRUITING	Integrates technical and cultural fit for recruiting based on performance prediction.
PhenomPeople	phenompeople.com	RECRUITING	Delivers candidate flow, customized experience, & short list through employer's website.
Pymetrics	pymetrics.com	RECRUITING	High-end assessment and performance prediction.
Salary.com	salary.com	COMPENSATION	Real time, demand based, market cognizant adjustment of compensation data.
Scout	goscoutgo.com	RECRUITING	Search firm management and recruiting marketplace.
SmartRecruiters	smartrecruiters.com	RECRUITING	Pattern detection for improved recruiting decisions.
Swoop	swooptalent.com	RECRUITING	Sourcing info. Extraordinary data mapping/integration intelligence.
TalentSonar	talentsonar.com	RECRUITING	Comprehensive intelligent recruiting workflow.
Talla	talla.com	BOT (EMPLOYEE)	Envisions bots as employees. HR product is designed to field benefits questions.
Textio	textio.com	RECRUITING	Augmented writing. More effective job descriptions.
Ultimate Software	ultimatesoftware.com	SPECTRUM	Blended quantitative and qualitative employee feedback as the foundation of HR/HCM.
WCN	wcn.uk	RECRUITING/SELECTION	College recruiting. Likelihood of interview/hire prediction.
Workday	workday.com	SPECTRUM	Building AI as a platform capability. Compelling vision.

RAW FUNCTIONALITY

COMPANY	Suite	Recruiting	L&D	Workforce Planning	Engagement/ Retention	Comp	Matching	Bot	HR General	Network Mapping	Data	Assessment
Bradio			x									
Burning Glass				x							x	
Ceridian	x				x		x		x			
Cornerstone on Demand	x	x	x		x		x					
Crowded		x									x	
Engage Talent		x			x							
Glint					x							
HireMya		x						x				
Hiretual		x										
HireVue		x					x					x
Humanyze										x		
IBM		x					x					x
Joberate		x			x							
Joyous					x							
karen.ai		x						x				
Koru		x										x
Kronos	x											
Leap.ai		x										
PhenomPeople		x					x					
Pymetrics		x										x
Salary.com						x						
Scout		x									x	
SmartRecruiters		x					x					
Swoop		x									x	
TalentSonar		x										x
Talla								x	x			
Textio		x										
Ultimate Software	x	x	x									
WCN		x										x
Workday	x	x	x				x					

Defining the Terrain

OVERVIEW

This report attempts to bring some order to the many claims and capabilities involving machine learning and artificial intelligence that are emerging in HR Technology. Far from being a monolithic universe with fixed categories, the Human Resources function (and its subsets) vary widely from organization to organization. The range and complexity of HR practices differ greatly by company size, industry, region, capital structure, and point in the organization's lifecycle.

We are entering a new era in software. Depending on whom you ask, it's the second or third era in the history of software. Yet, that discussion that is about as useful as defining the boundary lines between various generations in the workforce. Useful in theory, not so much in practice.

The emerging tools do much more than store data and format reports. While great breakthroughs in productivity and organizational operations were made possible by that form of early automation, what we are seeing today is different.

Yesterday's software was a lot like a spreadsheet. It came ready to be filled in and tailored to the customer's environment. The new tools begin with the assumption that the client has data. At their most excellent, they try to reduce the amount of time a client spends inside the application while multiplying the value they receive.

Multiple factors are accelerating the arrival of new tools and techniques. The dramatic movement of software to the cloud over the past decade is 50% complete (2017 Sierra Cedar Annual HR Systems Survey). As a result, the price of both data storage and processing dropped significantly. The major providers of those inexpensive commodity services (**Amazon, Oracle, Google**, and others) compete for clients by making increasingly better tools that use processing and data storage.

It's like the electric company developing lamps and light fixtures so people will buy electricity.

Nearly all the companies reviewed in this report use open source tools offered by cloud providers. (**WCN** is an exception).

The key here is that storage is all but free. Processing is cheap and available on demand. Tools for consuming these newly inexpensive commodities allow vendors to experiment with ideas that were prohibitively expensive a year or two ago.

The other important trend is that prediction, which is processing and storage intensive, is getting cheaper for the same reasons. As the availability of predictions has increased

20th century software has run its course. It's becoming hard to find an area of HR that is untouched by data hungry software monitoring processes and supporting tools. We are already starting to see comprehensive suites of tools that measure and account for the status of people, processes, and the intersections of both. That territory is mapped and covered.

The emerging products and services covered in this report transcend those foundational tools.

In the early days of Big Data, it was said that 'Data makes its own gravy.' That means that having data enables you to examine the data, and examining the data creates more data. With enough processing and enough data, you can see patterns that were never before visible. This is the foundation of this evolution of HRTech.

THE TECHNOLOGY

It is beyond the scope of this report to provide a comprehensive tutorial on the underlying technologies, but a few notes will make the terrain easier to navigate. If you are interested in a deeper look at the underlying tech, **HRExaminer** publishes a weekly list of 5 to 7 relevant links in a newsletter called the **HRIntelligencer**. The technology is rapidly evolving and the best way to stay on top of it is to have a constant stream of updates that keep you informed.

It is easy to feel overwhelmed by emerging technology. The great data scientists in our industry have PhDs from schools like Stanford, Berkeley, Carnegie Mellon, MIT, and the University of Toronto. A conversation with them about the operational details of their specialty is likely to make your head swim.

A surface level understanding should be enough to evaluate a given solution as long as the fundamental question remains: "How does this create business value?"

The following is intended to give the reader a simplified foundation for understanding the new technologies.

1. **Algorithm (or Model)**

    An algorithm is a set of rules and calculations. A non-automated procedural decision-making process (like levels of approval based on the dollars involved) can be considered algorithms. They can get extremely complex.

    For instance, the model that describes the interaction of every word in a resume with every other word in the resume and all of the words that may be related to each of those words is essentially beyond comprehension at a granular level. Still, it is an algorithm.

    Hyper-complex algorithms are often coupled with other expressions of data to form models of departments, companies, talent pools, and so on.

2. **Big Data (BD)**

    Companies like Amazon, Google, Apple, Facebook, Microsoft, eBay and the rest of the top 500 Websites have unimaginably huge sets of data. BD is a broad reference to the many tools used to analyze those data and discover underlying patterns. The evolution of Big Data over the past decade produced many of the tools that are currently being used to address HR problems.

There are only a few data sets in the HR universe that qualify as Big Data: all of job postings, all resumes in the word, the total volume of employee communications at companies with more that 100K employees, employee data at organizations with more than 250,000 employees (such as the US Department of Defense – 3.2M, The Chinese Military – 2.3M, Walmart – 2.1M, McDonald's – 1.9M, UK National Health Service – 1.7M).

In the rest of HR, the problems are somewhat different because the data sets are small by comparison. Some easy to execute techniques become slow and incomplete when there isn't enough data. The larger HR Tech firms (**Workday, Ultimate Software, Smart Recruiters, Kronos, IBM, Cornerstone On Demand, Ceridian**) may examine data across their client base to maximize the utility of Big Data tools. They often refer to this as benchmarking, but the process is more like a search for pattern repetition.

Big Data gathered across company lines in a client base always raises issues of confidentiality and privacy. At this point, the large players are all well versed in the nuances of these problems and have little difficulty ensuring that individual and company data is adequately isolated.

3. **Machine Learning (ML)**

    At its very essence, computing is composed of loops (repeated processes/algorithms) and counters. A counter tallies the number of times the loop completes itself. Sophisticated counters and loops handle variations and report the count as a distribution.

Once a primary analysis of a data set is complete, machine learning can go to work. The primary analysis unearths critical patterns, often prompted by a data scientist's hypotheses. From there, machine learning tools watch the evolution of patterns by counting and measuring their distributions.

For example, a flight risk analysis involves building a model of the patterns that are related to the likelihood that a given employee will leave (or that a specific department will experience attrition and how much). The various factors (time in grade, promotability, performance ratings, attendance, workload, overtime hours, and a host of others) are combined into a formula that scores the employee or department.

Each time an employee leaves, the math distributions are revised by the machine to reflect what happened. Each employee who stays also exerts an influence on the machine's view. Each new piece of data makes the machine recalculate the probability of what could happen next.

When ML systems are installed, they have some type of baseline estimates that are revised as the system gains specific experience. All ML tools that are installed in a unique environment have a learning curve. (Be sure to read the short chapter on latency)

4. **Natural Language Processing** (NLP)
   NLP is the sophisticated processing of text (and a significant subset of machine learning). It is used in a variety of ways to try to determine different kinds of meaning in documents. Sentiment Analysis identifies and categorizes opinions and emotions expressed in a piece of text.

NLP is also used to create significant alternatives to standard search. The use of word vectors to represent concepts allows you to submit the resume of your best engineer and have the search engine discover the best candidates like that engineer.

NLP is the primary tool used to create machine understanding of nuance and inference. Many words have multiple meanings. By building a library of associations with other words, machines begin to learn how to understand the meaning of a given phrase in a particular context.

5. **Bots/Chatbots**

A bot (short for robot) is an application that runs a series of automated scripts. These tools are used to collect data from around the internet or within a company's systems. Common types include spiders and web crawlers.

Chatbots are the most current variation of this technology. They are used to automate highly repeated process with observable answers. Chatbots generally have text interfaces (although voice based tools are coming rapidly).

The narrower the task, the better these tools perform. **HireMya** uses chatbots to sort and process the screening and hiring of low skilled hourly workers. The interview can be reduced to a decision tree so there is no misunderstanding. More complex levels of nuance lead to higher error rates.

Chatbots are one area where HR Technology can suffer from a shortage of transaction volume. It takes work to understand the various inferences in a dialog about HR issues. For now, complex chatbot installations in HR require a training and supervisory staff to handle high levels of error.

6. **Robotic Process Automation** (RPA)

    Tools like IFTT (ifttt.com) are simple, readily available script writing technologies that allow a user to link events in a process based on If-Then statements. That's the foundation of RPA – stringing together events in a process leading to a conclusion. It's desktop based processes where there is a clear decision tree.

Market Map

Intelligent technology is being applied to a variety of problems across the HR spectrum. Since it appears to be a fundamental capability of any application, the diversity of solutions is going to continue to grow, and that growth will accelerate. It is going to take some time, probably years, to fully comprehend the meaning and impact of this trend. t's already clear that the very definition of HR and the boundaries of traditional HR silos will shift significantly. For instance, recruiting, learning, and succession planning are currently treated as separate spheres because it's too hard to keep track of all of the moving parts.

That's an ideal job for an automated system that learns and monitors patterns.

Today's vendors are the early starters in a trend that will take 10 or 15 years to come to complete fruition. This early view of the market landscape combines what may seem like apples and oranges. The current state of things is that there is a lot of fruit. In other words, the categories are a bit hard to see. For an alternative view, see the 21 Use Cases Chapter which lists primary uses and the vendors who offer them.

It is worth repeating that these offerings are much more like laboratories working on an experiment than typical software offerings. The data scientists who lead each of the company projects are in a state of permanent innovation. The end result of their work may be a discovery that happens while they are answering a different question.

There are five wonderful examples of this in the current cohort of companies. In each case, there are enormous discoveries that happen in the process of refining the core business. If you speak with the leaders of these companies, they may well disagree with our assessment:

- **Crowded**

    Crowded devised and is perfecting a tool that refreshes the ATS candidate database with current information. There are myriad providers of that data and all of them have varying levels of quality and different times. The tool allows you to purchase the most current data for a given contact from all of the possible sources. The same problem exists throughout HR (particularly in employee data, competencies, skills definitions, compensation data, learning inventories and operational data).

- **EngageTalent**

    EngageTalent estimates the likelihood that a potential employee will respond to a call to talk about a new job. The core algorithm is a complex set of models rooted in current events, company specifics, personal history, career life cycle and so on. In order to continue to perfect the underlying algorithm, the company had to develop a comprehensive and accurate model of the distribution of tenure in all possible jobs. That sub-project is likely to be a product of its own.

- **Joberate**

    Joberate also makes flight risk predictions. They have converted social media signals into a lexicon of career signals, claiming to be able to infer career change behavior from intricate combinations of social media behavior.

- **Scout**

    Scout began as a marketplace for contingent search (3rd party) recruiters. As it matured, it discovered how to meld crowd-sourcing, ratings and single thread invoicing. It is the combination of services that makes it powerful.

- **SwoopTalent**

    SwoopTalent began its life as a sourcing tool. The idea was to build an application that allowed data from various sources to be uploaded to either the ATS or the CRM. Recruiters find and manufacture all sorts of data. To complete the project, they developed a tool that can integrate data sources without a pivot (or ID) column. Using NLP and a lot of processing, they are able to evaluate all of the data in the sources and identify commonalities on which to make the merge.

To date, the small scrappy startup has always had the advantage with new technology. The "Innovator's Dilemma" described the difficulties that hardware companies had seeing and responding to the next wave. The conventional wisdom is that a startup can beat an older company every time. That may not be true with this technical wave.

The incumbents all have a distinct advantage (depending on a few variables) because they have access to data. Large client bases and ongoing operations mean that large companies (generally platform providers of some type) have the data with which to train new tools that learn. Smaller companies usually don't. A few of the small companies will tell you that they spend significant parts of their resources figuring out how to build "fake data" for their systems to learn from. There are five long standing players covered by this report. Each is a strong technical provider with a distinct orientation. Individually, they are tacking the question of how to leverage the new material to improve the value their customers receive while reducing the amount of time spent in the application. It is not really possible to single out a "best in class" here. They are each headed down different roads.

- **Ceridian**

    Built on a core of payroll and workforce management, the Ceridian platform extends out into the rest of HR functionality. They are the most conservative marketers of their embedded technology. Effectively, they focus on the utilization of their massive databases of time, attendance, and pay info to predict flight risk and other workforce issues. They are pioneering the automation of new client configuration, reducing the cycle time to onboard their customers.

- **Cornerstone On Demand**

    The company began its life as a learning company and is building its intelligent technologies from the perspective of learning and recommendations for individual course paths. The company has a traditional pattern of innovating on a variety of fronts simultaneously and is doing so here.

- **Kronos**

    Kronos has its roots in workforce management and payroll. Its tools begin their life doing a sort of an audit orbit around the evolving database. That allows the system to spot patterns in a way that resembles fraud detection. One example is identifying supervisors who "trim" hourly timecards to meet weekly financial goals. Another involves offering improvements that increase shift effectiveness while a supervisor is scheduling.

- **Ultimate Software**

    The company is deeply committed to embedding employee feedback into work processes. It is a truism that the wisdom of the organization exists, often unharnessed, in the ranks of employees. In an effort that transcends anything that could possibly be called engagement, the firm is blending quantitative and qualitative feedback in a process that synthesizes the voice of the workforce while allowing individual input to come through. It is ground breaking.

- **Workday**

    Workday's core ethic involves making tools that customers can use to easily adapt to their operating environments. For that reason, they are building tools for data acquisition, prediction, and engagement into the heart of their platform. Workday has the most expansive vision of any of the platform providers of the long-range integration of HR, planning, and operations.

What is interesting is the degree to which the suite/ platform providers are differentiating based on their origins and strengths. It's a level of distinction between providers that has been challenging to find in recent years.

The bot providers show how broadly the tech can be applied. Each of the three bot services covered handle a different aspect of HR and Recruiting. As the inference problem (see the Terrain chapter) responds to innovation, bot style interfaces in text, voice, and video will proliferate. These are the early examples:

- **Talla**

    Talla positions itself as a provider of digital employees and is the most ambitious, far reaching of the bot services.

- **Karen.ai**

    Karen.ai is a "recruiting assistant" and shares some functionality with Hiretual (which is a data laden web service with no particular interface intelligence.) The idea is to simplify recruiting processes through automation.

- **HireMya**

    HireMya is a text based bot that filters basic yes or no questions in the process of engaging hourly laborers. It's an example of how powerful the tech can be in properly constrained environments.

The other large grouping involves using some sort of assessment to solve questions of employee fit.

- **HireVue:** uses video interviews as a data source combined with traditional I/O assessment.

- **IBM:** Based on mountains of historic data from the 20th century I/O model channeled through Watson.

- **Koru:** focused on soft skills with performance predictions.

- **Leap.ai:** Cultural fits in Silicon Valley.

- **Phenom People:** Tailors company employment website experience to cull volume candidates.

- **Pymetrics:** Gamified traditional I/O assessment.

- **Talent Sonar:** Designed to eliminate bias towards African Americans, Women, Latinos and Latinas.

- **Textio:** Helps reshape job descriptions to attract specific types of people, reducing bias.

- **WCN:** Structured data used to predict hiring in high volume settings.

The biggest surprise would be if there were no entrants focused on performance management and other forms of employee-employer communications.

- **Glint:** a more traditional pulse and engagement survey company driven by pattern recognition and smart analytics.

- **Joyous:** Experimenting with the idea that all aspects of employee communications are a part of the same conversation. Applies smart tech to synthesizing relevant trends.

The diversity of the remaining entrants signals the coming changes in HR and HR Tech.

- **Braidio:** Deep learning in a very high volume single product call center environment.

- **Burning Glass:** Synthesizing skills data from massive quantities of job positions and using it as the basis for workforce planning.

- **Humanyze:** Measuring and monitoring employee behavior.

- **Salary.com:** Real time data quality control in complex databases.

- **SmartRecruiters:** Process improvement in recruiting.

The following market map organizes the players by the likelihood that they will have access to a mass market and solve an actual business problem. All of the companies are in a position to make money from their work. In some cases, a tiny niche is a profitable niche. Braidio is a good example of this. In other cases, like the assessment companies, a small niche is only profitable if you trim your ambition.

MARKET MAP

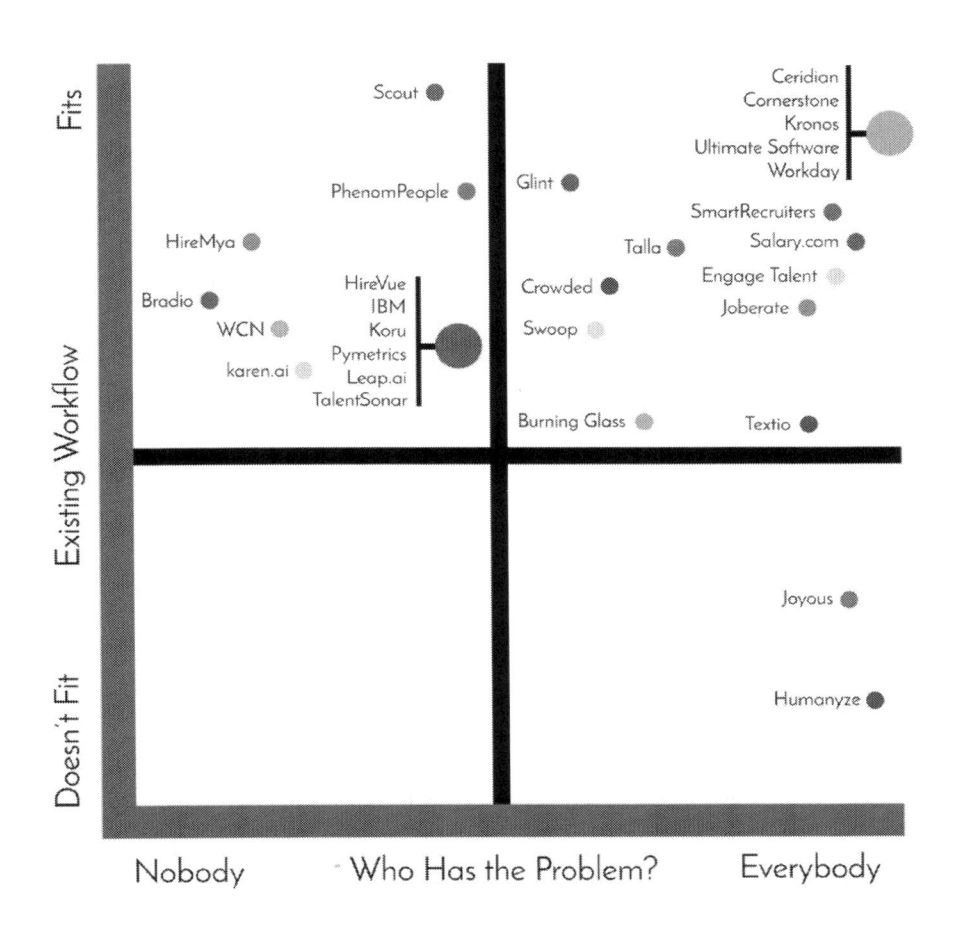

(Y-axis: Fits / Existing Workflow / Doesn't Fit; X-axis: Nobody — Who Has the Problem? — Everybody)

Upper-left quadrant (Fits / Nobody):
- Scout
- PhenomPeople
- HireMya
- Bradio
- WCN
- karen.ai
- HireVue
- IBM
- Koru
- Pymetrics
- Leap.ai
- TalentSonar

Upper-right quadrant (Fits / Everybody):
- Ceridian
- Cornerstone
- Kronos
- Ultimate Software
- Workday
- Glint
- SmartRecruiters
- Talla
- Salary.com
- Crowded
- Engage Talent
- Joberate
- Swoop
- Burning Glass
- Textio

Lower-right quadrant (Doesn't Fit / Everybody):
- Joyous
- Humanyze

27

Ethical Considerations

"Enterprise software product liability"

Those four words make some people very uncomfortable. For the entire life of the software industry, people have not been concerned about product liability. The issues were covered in the license agreements and terms and conditions, and generally absolved the software companies from liability for everything but basic warranties that the software would run.

Today, things are changing.

The first era of software stretched from ballistic tables and payroll to the latest in HR Forms completion. Over the course of 80 years, software recorded, collected, calculated, and reported data. GIGO (Garbage In, Garbage Out) was the primary principle. There could be no liability because machines simply reported what they were given.

In this second era, machines are doing more than just reporting. Some of today's tools (and all of tomorrow's) do much more than record, process, and report. They suggest, recommend, decide, evaluate, prescribe, filter, analyze, monitor, and learn. Era 1 tools could not hurt people. Era 2 tools can. In a world where machines extract truth and insight, they (at least) share responsibility for the decisions the cause. It may be that they are completely responsible.

One leading industry CEO says, "we call it machine learning when we talk about it internally. We call it artificial intelligence when we speak to the market." For the purposes of this article, I'll use the terms Machine Learning, Artificial Intelligence, and Big Data somewhat interchangeably. I am referring to our computers' emerging ability to change their output based on insights derived from new data.

HR Enterprise Software tools will be at the forefront of the implementation of new product liability concerns. Increasingly, HR software recommends and directs the behavior of managers and employees. If the guidance or insight is damaging or wrong, software vendors may be unable to wriggle out from the consequences.

Currently, the vast majority of recommendations provided by intelligent HR software are 'self-correcting.' They learn from their mistakes and correct the underlying world view. It is common to hear them described as tools that 'get better with usage.' Another way of saying that is that their error rate improves over time. One part of the liability issue is the question, who bears responsibility for the error rate?

There is a more difficult dimension.

All cultures, organizational or otherwise, are defined by their biases. The essence of culture is its unique world view. Decisions and behaviors that support and expand the world view are rewarded. Things that undermine or contradict the worldview receive negative feedback.

Since algorithmic decision-making adjusts to the things that make a culture different, they tend to amplify the biases of the culture. Most of these machine learning tools are black boxes. The only way to see the bias is by examining the output. In other words, these new tools may create liability before it can be discovered and managed.

Intelligent machines (and wonderful theories about their near and long term potential) are at the heart of today's pop culture. Everyone 'knows' that self-driving cars are just around the corner, that robots are going to take your job, and that pretty soon you'll be talking to an intelligent assistant who knows where you put your car keys and can order more laundry detergent.

Yet, these programs and machines are not people who are generally governed by standards of reasonable care. They are property, which is governed by laws of strict product liability, warranty, and whether the design is fit for the intended use. The difference is much like an owner's liability when their dog bites someone. The dog is a separate actor, the owner did not intend for the dog to harm anyone, but the owner is strictly liable because the dog is the owner's property.

We are seeing companies develop and sell technology based on machine learning processes that the human designers do not fully understand nor control. These machines are giving recommendations and suggestions based on probabilities to employees, many of whom are ill equipped to understand and effectively use the information. Often, we don't know whether the information will be useful until we develop and test it over time.

But it's not just data. It's evidence. And the laws that will apply are not the ones that organizations have traditionally been operating under. There is a chain of potential liability that runs from the developer vendors through the sales chain to the organizations using the software and machines.

Not surprisingly, HR has been slow to adopt AI and Machine learning technologies.

The Sierra-Cedar HR Technology Industry survey suggests that fewer that 7% of the companies they surveyed are using or considering using Machine Learning technologies in HR.

Given that we are at the earliest of early adopter stages, it's a solid time to think about the ethics involved in using machine learning systems to manage, supervise, assess, train, deploy, or categorize human beings.

Ethics involves questions of right and wrong. Large institutions are usually concerned with optimization, efficiency, and innovation. They seek ways to maximize returns and minimize costs. They think of their employees as resources first and people second. Corporations have traditionally had some challenges with the very idea of ethics.

Here are the kinds of ethics questions that are going to occupy the conversation about ethics in HR Technology. The questions are standard. The answers may vary from place to place.

- **Who owns employee data**? Who can sell or manipulate it? How much is an employee entitled to see? If something is wrong, what recourse does the employee have? If it is embedded in some machine learning scheme, what are the ownership variables?

- **If the system learns about itself through data about an employee, does the employee own the learning**? Can she take it with her when she goes? Is she entitled to royalties if the data is sold for benchmarking or other purposes.?

- **Is it okay to use data that was built without a control group**? How do we measure effectiveness in the example of experimental control? When machines improve their error rate while implemented in an organization are there extra employee protections required?

- **What is the line between manipulation and motivation**? If chatbots increase emotional ties, is it okay to use them to increase engagement scores? What are the likely regulatory responses to overly manipulative work environments? Don't people usually follow orders from authority figures? Doesn't this apply to machines? Is there a limit to self-congratulatory positive feedback?

- **Are statistics more reliable than human decision-making**? Where's the proof? Are empathy and compassion necessary for the decision? How about kindness, understanding, or generosity? Humans are also demonstrably more effective at handling novel and/or erratic inputs to decision making. Does that matter? How do you factor unmeasurables into the decision-making process?

- **How do you disagree with a machine's decisions?** Can you afford to be the person who is carping about decision quality? How do you get into a position to see bias? It won't show up in individual recommendations, it's systemic. Do we get stupid in the face of a machine recommendation? Are people predisposed to follow the instructions of an authority figure? Consider Google Maps and one's ability to argue with its recommendations.

- **Who has the liability for machine recommendations?** Who pays for damage caused by the machine? How do you handle mistakes? How do you monitor the quality of the algorithm's performance? Is it ethical to use tools that are known to be imperfect on employees? Are there implicit human experiences that are interfered with when machines are the arbiters of personnel decisions?

- **How do you limit the data's ability to influence the company?** How do you turn it off and replace it? How do you know when you have too much influence from a single source? Are there tools that allow you to see the risk in machine led decisions?

In a nutshell, the ethics questions we will be grappling with are rooted in the fact that we simply don't understand in a sophisticated way:

- How human beings work
- How organizations work
- How the human-machine interface will change these things.

We are going to learn more about each issue in an accelerated way. The machines are coming to employment decisions, and we will learn from their mistakes and successes. You can expect to discover new ways of thinking about employee safety as the risks at work shift from physical to mental and emotional.

If you are considering the utilization of intelligent machines in your HR/Operations processes, here are some questions you might consider.

- **Tell me about your views on product liability**

    Be sure to have a long conversation about how the tool works and how the vendor is monitoring the impact of machine learning curves. You'll learn a lot by raising the topic of product liability. Most vendors still imagine that we are in the first generation of software where liability is not really a possibility. The key question here is: What if your tool's recommendations cause damage to people or our business?

- **How do we make changes to the historical data?**

    Most machine learning systems are 'black boxes.' If you ask the designers how they work, they can only explain about 80%. That means that you are likely to want to modify the results that the machine produces. It is likely that the answer to this question is 'you can't.' Having the conversation is what's important. It will give you a window on your real risks.

- **What happens when we turn "it" off? How much notice will we receive if you turn it off?**

    Imagine that you are using a tool that does the job of several employees (sourcers who review resumes, for example). If the tool fails in a way that requires a shutdown, what sort of advance warning do you get. Since most providers are in experimental stages, the answer to this question also matters if the project ceases to operate. In a very real way, these are digital workers and it is best to have a replacement plan.

- **Do we own what the machine learned from us? How do we take that data with us?**
- Part of the way that these systems operate is that they learn in both the aggregate and individual case. Most vendors guarantee that your data is 'anonymized'. You still may not wish to have your operating practices be a part of some larger benchmarking process after you change suppliers. Being very clear about whether the system will retain evidence of your participation after you go is of strategic import.

- **What are the startup costs, resources, and supervision?**
We know precious little about the behavior of intelligent machines. There is good reason to expect that their impact on your resource consumption is greater than anyone thinks today. Like any employee, they require training, supervision and discipline. Make sure you have a very clear picture of the Total Cost of Ownership of any leaning machine you enable.

The age of human-machine integration is in its infancy. It is inevitable. In the transition, it is important that we move forward carefully with a clear picture of the risks and ethical issues. This note is a starting point.

Latency

Latency is the difference between the real world and what the machine thinks the real world is. More formally, it's the time between stimulation and response. In software that learns, it is the amount of time it takes a machine to understand the current environment.

Most systems that tailor themselves to a customer's culture or procedures have an embedded learning curve. The vendors who provide these services often speak of a learning period that ranges from 60 days to a year. The real distance, however, is some number of transactions.

The number of transactions (or amount of learning) required to have a system effectively reflect a customer's present-day values, processes, and policies is a little hard to pin down. I did not talk with a vendor who could clearly articulate the distance, in time or transactions, between the current state of the machine and the current state of the organization.

In fact, none of the vendors had considered that organizations are dynamic entities that change routinely. The following kinds of major happenings shift organizational behavior:

- CEO transitions
- leadership changes
- mergers &acquisitions
- stock price volatility
- layoffs
- rapid growth
- life cycle transitions
- new product launches
- disruption

- market pressure
- external political changes
- reorganizations
- attrition rate variations
- external economic circumstances
- capital structure of the firm
- new technology
- redesigned processes
- financial performance

Each of these factors has a significant influence on how people fit into the organization and how the organization responds to various levels of effort. Today, we are just learning how to measure and understand the impact of these variables on operations, productivity, human capital utilization, employment branding, engagement, and employee experience.

It is easy for a machine that learns from decisions made by the company to fall behind. The human beings are learning the new terrain and have their own learning curve. The machine's learning inherently follows the path that the humans take. At each of these inflection points, the machine falls behind and takes some time to catch up. The process is anything but instantaneous.

Worse yet, the pace of change is accelerating making it impossible to really understand where the machine is on its learning curve. There are no currently observable tools for delivering a full assessment of the state of the machine. Currently, no vendor promises more than 80% or 90% accuracy in the performance of their tool.

Talla, the bot company includes an error correction process in order to guarantee performance. Google offers **Chatbase** (chatbase.com), a chatbot analytics tool that allows you to see the depths of the latency problem in a chatbot. There are currently no tools for examining these sorts of alignment issues in assessment, resume matching, cultural measures, or the performance of machine recommendations.

The lag between recommendations and results is not a new problem. HR has always suffered from a feedback loop that stretches over the course of a year or more. Automating that process will definitely make it more consistent. We simply don't know whether that additional consistency is useful and have no data to prove the case either way.

Jobs are not static things. They evolve as the company learns and the technology changes. They shift when they are outsourced. They can be declared irrelevant. They get merged. They obsolesce. The people doing the jobs get smarter and do different things for better results. Any tool that views the job as a static thing is subject to significant latency problems.

The hardest to fill jobs are constantly evolving. What makes a software developer an asset today makes her a liability in a year. The requirements for the job are constantly changing. A resume matching process that utilizes last year's job description will inherently have a latency problem.

The same logic applies anywhere the machine is covering something that changes from employee policies to benefits choices from managerial decision making to recruiting automation. Managers who take on digital employees that learn will have to be able to measure, articulate and repair the latency problems those tools exhibit.

5 Key Questions to consider when designing or buying intelligent software:

1. How long does it take the machine to learn something new? Can you define that both in calendar time and the number of transactions?

2. What are the feedback loops we should use to monitor the tool's alignment with our culture, processes, and procedures?

3. What is the process by which we inform the device that it is missing something or needs to learn something new?

4. If the machine makes a recommendation and we think it's out of date, what do we do?

5. What sort of staff do we need to ensure the performance of our intelligent software?

Total Cost of Ownership (TCO)

It's tempting to think that buying a piece of software is all that there is to it. Often, other costs outstrip the costs of licenses and a little tech support.

Item	Bot	Point Solution	Suite
Initial Project Plan/Requirements	x	x	x
Initial License/Support	x	x	included
Data Cleaning/Restructuring	x	x	depends
Initial Content Creation (answers)	x	x	depends
Initial Content Creation (Questions/Inference)	x	x	depends
Content Maintenance (Small Transitions, anomalies)	x	x	x
Refresh After Large Transition	x	x	x
Understanding and Meeting Performance Expectations	x	x	x
The cost of learning (startup)	x	x	x
Staffing to solve exceptions	x	x	x

The most important question you can ask when considering the adoption of some form of process automation is: "How many people will it take to staff this project properly?". Today (late 2017), we have only small bits of data about the complexity of predictive/prescriptive projects. Unbridled optimism and the urge to be an early adopter may make it hard to see the full implications of the costs of implementation and execution of some of these products.

One thing is reasonably clear: in the system you are considering, the difference between forecast accuracy and 100% will be depend on headcount from your department and productive time lost elsewhere in the organization. If the chatbot answers 80% of the questions posed to it, a human team will still have to answer the rest. If the recruiting hireability prediction is 80%, humans will still need to drive it to a decision.

Here are the fundamental elements of cost/ budget you'll have to account for and consider:

- **Initial Requirements Definition/Project Scope**

  Most of the emerging solutions don't exactly solve specific problems that you currently have. In other words, most point solutions/chatbots are not designed to fit seamlessly into your existing workflow. Each requires that you rethink your existing process in order to harvest the benefits that they offer. In other words, every installation of new functionality will require a change management program.

  Although this is less true with suite based solutions, new processes and inputs require new policies and some sort of test methodology. For example, it is unwise to simply release 'flight risk data' to everyone in the organization. Rather, you'll need to control the levels of distribution and create quantitative policy.

  Every new intelligence infused process or tool requires careful consideration before implementation. The initial planning may become quite expensive.

- **Initial License/Support**

  This is probably the most straightforward part of the budget. It will be important to pin down key performance measures for support. The object of the project is the delivery of measurable results, not the acquisition of software and service.

- **Data Cleaning/Restructuring**

  Clean data is the foundation of all useful predictive/prescriptive projects. Unless the new process is directly focused on fixed, separate information (resumes, FAQs, written policies/procedures), aligning data elements is a foundational problem.

Any time data is required from multiple sources, a time-consuming process of data aggregation and governance ensues. The implications range from standardizing workflows to agreeing to data element labels. In a complex organization with multiple competing systems of record, this work can take as long as a year. Tools like SwoopTalent are emerging to make connecting disparate data easier.

Still, effective analytics, predictions, and prescriptions can only come from standardized processes. A surprising amount of work can be required to cause the existing data to conform to the requirements for predictive tools. It is best to thoroughly review data quality requirements with your vendor in advance of any purchase decision.

Often, facing the problem causes the organization to decide to adopt suite technology. Expect to see a migration from best of breed solutions to the new suites as data cleaning burdens begins to emerge.

- **Initial Content Creation (Answers)**

  Any bot implementation depends entirely on having an inventory of all of the answers the bot needs to give. While this is a simple requirement to articulate, and it's the easiest part of bot implementation, taking the time to have a comprehensive set of answers can take significant time and resources because each customer's questions and answers will be somewhat different.

  In many cases, this is as simple as porting the company FAQ's to the bot's format. Unfortunately, a fair number of the people who hope to utilize bots simply don't have those FAQs. So, for them, the cost of implementation is the cost of building those FAQs on top of everything else.

Tools like Mya work well because they completely minimize the scope that the bot has to cover. Constraining scope and expectations is a perfect way to manage the TCO.

- **Initial Content Creation (Questions/Inference)**

The hardest part of content creation involves getting the questions right. Where the pile of answers is finite, the pile of questions is infinite. A simple example is a question about bereavement leave.

The answer to the question is 'Our bereavement leave is three days leave plus expenses for putting your pets in a kennel.' The questions could include:
    - My father just passed, what can I do?
    - How long can I take off under the bereavement policy?
    - Can I take time off to go to a funeral?
    - Do my benefits include cremation coverage for my wife?
    - Am I allowed to go to the service for my Mom?
    - My brother wants to move from hospice to die at home. Can I take time off to care for him? (Which may also implicate FMLA.)

Death is a particularly tricky subject because it is taboo in many ways that are culture-dependent. But, the same logic applies to bots that exist to answer employment branding questions or to help navigate other processes and procedures.

For any interactive system to be useful, it must be able to infer meaning so that it can provide answers. The 'inference problem' is largely unsolved at this point. That means that all systems that communicate answers will have limits to their effectiveness.

- **Content Maintenance (Small Transitions/Anomalies)**
  Bots and intelligent systems are not mind readers. They have to be informed about changes in the organization and policies that they are charged with navigating. A job matching system has to be informed about changes to the job description. A benefits bot must be told when providers or offerings change.

  Every organizational system encounters anomalies that skew results, such as this year's weather changes and attendance patterns, a competitor causes a workforce disruption, the local team wins a championship, an important politician's visit disrupts quarterly revenue, or the boss' children all get promotions. The potential for anomalies is endless and often unpredictable.

  All data used by a machine to understand future behavior need to be groomed to exclude observable anomalies that will skew its recommendations. The team that administers the system must have these capabilities and anticipate adjustments and make them. They usually don't.

- **Refresh After Large Transitions**
  All companies go through changes in leadership, ownership, strategy, products, business models, and sales approaches. Mergers, acquisitions, dispositions, layoffs, and surge hiring also produce waves of change. Each of these changes requires a minimum of a review and includes the possibility that the learning process must be restarted.

- **Defining/Meeting Performance Expectations**

    In the earliest stages of a project to utilize machine intelligence in decision making, it is imperative that you define and understand the level of accuracy you will be expecting. Long term adoption of the system will be dependent on effective setting of service expectations. It is reasonable to expect that the early stages of system operation will require extensive human assistance.

    Don't bet project success on the notion that the technology will work perfectly. Expect that your team will make up the difference between the expectations you set and whatever the technology delivers.

- **The Cost of Learning (Startup)**

    Every intelligent system has an initial learning curve. Depending on the project and its complexity, coming up to speed will take between 60 days and a year. The actual timeline will depend more on transaction volume that calendar time.

    This is the time that it takes for the new system to understand the ins and outs of your organization. Human care and attention (particularly for unexpected situations) will consume a lot of resources. Budget as if you were about to train a very smart four-year-old.

- **Staffing to Solve Exceptions**

    Every new machine decision-making system should have a trouble ticket process. When the bot doesn't answer the question properly or an executive disagrees with a recommendation, there should be a 'trouble ticket' process in place with turn around guarantees and human beings in charge of fixing the problem.

This should give you a rough sense of the time and resources that are really required to implement an intelligent tool. The bad news is that these variables are all uncertain for early adopters. The good news is that early adopters reap the lion's share of benefits from new technology.

21 Common Use Cases

The following table attempts to characterize the 21 most common use cases presented by the thirty vendors in this study. While there is lots of overlap at level of raw functionality, each vendor solves the problem in a unique way.

For example, **BurningGlass**, **Textio,** and **TalentSonar** all address job description/posting efficacy, they do it in radically different ways. **BurningGlass** examines skills currency in the market and applies that to make a job description more relevant to business needs. **Textio** examines the impact of the language of a description/posting on audiences and attraction. **TalentSonar** focuses exclusively on reducing bias towards Women, African Americans, Latinas, and Latinos.

One could conceivably use all three tools simultaneously.

Only a few of the vendors offer single use cases (**EngageTalent**, **HireMya**, **Humanyze**, **Joberate**, **Talla**). Single use tends to suggest that they dig deeper into their fundamental question. HireVue, who have been around longer than most, only recently expanded into a more powerful set of questions

It's been apparent throughout the report that larger, older, more complex companies have an advantage based on the depth of their data (**Ceridian**, **CornerstoneOnDemand**, **HireVue**, **Kronos**, **IBM**, **Salary.com**, **SmartRecruiters**, **Ultimate Software**, **Workday**). That seems to express as a wider range of use cases.

Traditionally, large spectrum providers have provided less depth in their offerings while point solutions went deeper. That doesn't seem to hold perfectly in this cohort. Small operations searching for market relevance (sales) seem to expand the breadth of their offerings while the companies mentioned above are focused and going deeper.

	Use Case	Techniques	Vendors
1	**Assessment**: Define success characteristics, measure people against them, present rank ordered lists.	ML/NLP	HireVue, Koru, Leap.ai, PhenomPeople, Pymetrics, TalentSonar, WCN
2	**Selection Bias Reduction**: Minimize (sometimes promise to remove) human tendencies to choose people who share the chooser's characteristics.	ML/NLP	Cornerstone On Demand, HireVue, IBM, Koru, Leap.ai, PhenomPeople, Pymetrics, Salary.com, SmartRecruiters, TalentSonar, Ultimate Software, Workday
3	**Broad based enterprise improvements**: Using existing data to examine ongoing processes and audit/recommend/improve those processes.	ML/NLP	Ceridian, Cornerstone on Demand, Kronos, SmartRecruiters, Ultimate Software, Workday
4	**Communicating HR policies/benefits**: Replace human call centers with digital employees.	Bot	Talla
5	**Data Freshness Assurance**: Automated data maintenance in settings where accuracy means timeliness.	ML/NLP	Crowded, Salary.com, SwoopTalent
6	**Data Manipulation/Marketplace**: Big Data-ish projects to unearth insight from large volumes of data or high volume flows.	ML/NLP	BurningGlass, Crowded, Scout, SwoopTalent, Textio, Salary.com
7	**Edge Learning and Productivity Acceleration in Large Call Centers**: Transmits knowledge rapidly in real time for rapid productivity gains.	ML	Bradio
8	**Employee Availability (Flight Risk)**: Measures and assesses the likelihood that a person will leave their job.	NL/NLP	Ceridian, Cornerstone on Demand, EngageTalent, Joberate, Ultimate Software, Workday,
9	**Employment Website Automation**: Candidate experience customization, matching, traffic acquisition.	ML/NLP	PhenomPeople
10	**Embedded Ongoing Process Audits (Payroll, Scheduling)**: Processes that identify potential risks, fraud, and offer solutions.	ML/NLP	Ceridian, Crowded, Kronos
11	**Engagement, Employee Communications**: Communication flows featuring either formal surveys or sentiment analysis.	ML/NLP	Glint, Joyous, Ultimate Software
12	**Implementation**: Automation of complex manual implementation processes by predicting the required configuration based on similar cases.	ML/NLP	Ceridian, Workday
13	**Integrated Workforce Planning**: Workflow from Future scenarios through recruiting accountability with talent trend analysis.	ML/NLP	BurningGlass
14	**Job Description Transformation/ Performance Prediction**: Improve the effectiveness of job postings/job descriptions by improving language or skills descriptions.	ML/PNLP	BurningGlass, TalentSonar, Textio,
15	**Network Mapping and Monitoring**: Measure and track digital and physical behavior to disclose the way work actually happens.	ML/NLP	Humanyze
16	**Operational Excellence**: Focus on making software that takes less time to perform functions while producing more value.	ML/NLP	Ceridian, Humanyze, Kronos, Salary.com, SmartRecruiters, Workday
17	**Performance Prediction**: Uses resume or assessment tool to forecast employee fit/performance.		HireVue, IBM, Koru, Leap.ai, PhenomPeople, Pymetrics, TalentSonar, WCN
18	**Recruiting Assistant**: Multiple functions from scheduling and contact info acquisition to communications flow.	Bot	Hiretual, Karen.ai
19	**Resume Matching**: Compares job description with resumes to winnow down large piles of resumes.	ML/NLP	Ceridian, Cornerstone on Demand, Hiretual, HireVue, IBM, Koru, Leap.ai, PhenomPeople, Pymetrics, SmartRecruiters, TalentSonar, Ultimate Software, WCN, Workday
20	**Text Augmentation**: Scores and gamifies the improvement of documents (begins with job descriptions but can be utilized throughout HR).	ML/ NLP	Textio
21	**Text Based Screening and Processing of Low Skill Hourly Workers**: Friction elimination in non-smartphone high volume/rapid demand recruiting processes.	Bot	HireMya

Forecasts

These are the early days. The transformation of HR software into something smarter and more lively is just beginning. We are about to learn unimaginable things.

- Current modeling and prediction methods (including the technologies covered in this report) are extremely rigid. The early days of adoption will have an authoritarian feel to them. Machine recommendations will seem harsh in retrospect.

- The cost of prediction is falling rapidly. The most sought after skill in the coming years will be the ability to combine diverse predictions into a course of action. The net result of the initial experiments in machine decisions will be greater demands on human decision making.

- The automobile was invented by Karl Benz. In its first public outing it crashed. It took many years to build the kinds of roads that became our transportation system. This wave of technology will have those sorts of accidents and cause significant transformation to work itself.

- We will come to understand our new digital employees as less capable than their human counterparts. They require training, supervision, remedial learning, and extensive monitoring and maintenance. They are more literal minded than any human employee. Changes, even small ones, confuse and bewilder them.

- Over time, the ambitions of the technology designers will transcend the solution to current problems. Contemporary funding mechanisms (venture capital) require a focus on practical deliverables at the expense of vision.

Ultimately though, these tools will reshape HR, what it does, and how things are done.

- The idea that recruiting, learning, performance management, organizational development, change management, payroll, benefits, and workforce planning are distinct disciplines is a creation of 20th century specialization. It was a necessary part of the first wave of software development. These categories will no longer apply.

- It's possible that there is a limit to the speed at which people can make decisions, that organizations can only move so fast. We will have some problems caused by the rapidly increasing rate of decision making capabilities led by machine recommendations.

- Machine recommendations will be largely understood as decision from the very beginning. That will result in a significant range of misplaced bets. The tools we need to manage our new helpers will emerge as the result of mistakes. Some of those mistakes could be significant. Almost all of them will affect human lives. To go with these new capabilities, we will also need the machine equivalent of bumpers, guard rails, airbags, seat belts, lane markings, stop lights, and curbs.

- Human replacements for HR practitioners will be a long time coming. The discipline often requires subtlety and nuance. It will be many years before machines acquire these traits.

- One of the most interesting impending calamities will involve recruiting. As the pace of technical change accelerates, the idea that a job is a static thing that can be treated like an object (or a product) will prove to have been a shallow view (and largely responsible for the dreadful rate of recruiting success). We will see a number of cases of business failure brought on by hiring people who perfectly met the requirements for a job.

- Jobs are technical expressions of a social network. The work and the worker have to fit in the complete organizational framework. We have barely scratched the surface in our understanding of how this organic process actually works. The full capability of intelligent systems can't be realized until we can adequately articulate their operational context. This is the work of decades.

- We don't really know whether the 'routine, mundane work' we are starting to automate is important. It is possible that doing simple repetitive things is the best way to develop new workers. If it's automated, we may have a major training challenge.

- It is very hard to argue with a machine. They have all the data.

Companies We Didn't Cover This Time

The machine learning/artificial intelligence category is exploding. Since this is the next generation of software, you can expect many more vendors to emerge, particularly where intelligence can be embedded in software with readily available tools.

That means we are headed into an era of extreme and interesting innovation. HR technology silos will consolidate and disappear. Most importantly, the number of choices facing a buyer will expand exponentially.

This table is a list of the companies we want to get to in the next edition of the report. We didn't cover them this time for a number of reasons, usually because:

- They declined to participate because they weren't ready or weren't interested;
- We didn't discover them soon enough; or
- They made their market entry while we were doing the research.

In addition to the names on this list, you can be certain that there will be intelligent entries from every incumbent vendor in the HRTech ecosystem. The pressure to deliver more value with less time in the application will be immense.

If you know of a company that should be covered. Please let us know.

Company	Website	Focus	Nutshell
AbilityMap	abilitymap.com	Recruiting	Performance prediction in people and jobs
ADP	adp.com	Spectrum	Data giant. Lots of potential for AI/predictive
aptozen	aptozen.com	Recruiting	Predictive hiring insights
Arya	goarya.com	Recruiting	Automated Recruiting, mover predictor
Aurion	aurion.com	Recruiting	HRIS
Axonify	axonify.com	Learning	Deconstructed intelligent learning featuring micro-learning
beamery	beamery.com	Recruiting	Candidate relationship software
brilent	brilent.com	Recruiting	Automatically identify high value candidates
CareerBuilder	careerbuilder.com	Recruiting	Recruiting Platform
Dataminr	dataminr.com	Recruiting	Real time information newsfeed
Entelo	entelo.com	Recruiting	Candidate recommendations from social media
Gilder	gilder.ai	Recruiting	"Recruit top talent with AI"
GoHire	gohire.com	Recruiting	Chatbot. Claims AI
Greenhouse	greenhouse.io	ATS	Predictive analytics in Recruiting
HiQ Labs	hiqlabs.com	Recruiting	Flight risk analysis. Skills deconstruction from job postings.
HiringSolved	hiringsolved.com	Recruiting	Smart people aggregator RAI: first AI Assistant
Human Predictions	humanpredictions.io	Recruiting	Using public data to predict flight risk
ideal	ideal.com	Recruiting	Bot "AI for Recruiting" Virtual Assistant
Intervyo	intervyo.com	Recruiting	Virtual interviewer
JobJet	jobjet.com	Recruiting	Contact info consolidator
Knockri	knockri.com	Video Interviewing	Video Interviewing as Data Collection
Lever	lever.co	ATS	Predictive analytics in Recruiting
LinkedIn	linkedin.com	Recruiting	Embedded intelligence
Oracle	Oracle.com	Spectrum	Some rumblings about 'auditable AI', understandable black boxes
Pulsifi	pulsifi.me	Talent Management	Staff, Retain and Develop Talent w/ AI
Recruiting.ai	Recruiting.ai	Recruiting	Bot. Olivia
Sap	successfactors.com	Spectrum	In management transition
SignalHire	signalhire.com	Recruiting	Predictive candidate availability
Stella	stella.ai	Recruiting	Generate a pre-qualified slate of candidates for any open job
Symphony	symphonytalent.com	Talent Management	Platform
textrecruit	textrecruit.com	Recruiting	Chatbot
UIPath	uipath.com	General	Task automation
Uncommon	uncommon.co	Recruiting	Improved job candidate search and ad creation platform
Wade & Wendy	http://wadeandwendy.ai/	Recruiting	helps you find jobs and hire people
WeAreHuman	wearehuman.io/#sectionseven	Assessment	Capture and analyze human feelings

Appendix: Company Pages

BRADIO

Braidio was founded in 2011 in San Francisco. Founder Iain Scholnick is an ex rugby player who maintains the rugged determination and grit of the sport. That makes him an unusual member of the L&D ecosystem.

Bradio solves one problem with abandon.

Imagine that you operate a call center that supports customers with smart phones. Each year when the models emerge, 10 or 20 Millions of your customers need support over the course of a two hour call. That's 20 Million labor hours (or 10,000 people doing the exact same job).

Here's the thing about new phones (or whatever the technical product.) The problems experienced by the field cannot be understood until they are experienced. In other words, the 10,000-person workforce faces the new product with almost no understanding of what the actual problems will be.

As the collective team interacts with the customer base, several things begin to happen. Customer support begins to be able to see clusters of support issues and the call center team begins to discover the solutions to the problems. In order to rapidly reduce costs and optimize system performance, the question is how to move discoveries from individuals to the larger group and how to prioritize that delivery.

This is an environment where the speed of knowledge acquisition yields direct benefit to the bottom line. If you discover a simple answer to a 20-minute problem that every user is having, you can save 15 minutes times 10M calls. That's 150 Million minutes, 2.5 Million hours or $50M dollars per year.

In other words, learning in this sort of organization has real financial payoff.

Braidio is a learning accelerator. It's goal; as a [product is to deliver Just In Time information as soon as it is available. It allows individual contributors to learn in ways that can be aggregated like crown sourcing. The system then figures out how to prioritize the learning on an individual basis.

Humans have a maximum learning throughput capacity. In large call centers, part of the prioritization problem has to do with making sure that each employee's learning provides maximum benefit. As Braidio learns about the organization, it is able to see where learning can be applied for maximum system benefit.

The Braidio tool is one of the most exciting innovations covered by this survey.

BURNING GLASS TECHNOLOGIES (B)

There are very few problems in HR that merit the title 'Big Data'. B is one of a few companies who are tackling the most noticeable pile of big data: the huge volume of job posting data. The company has built an impressive business in the Education industry by condensing hundreds of millions of job postings into intelligent data about supply and demand in the labor market.

The most important thing that any company can do in the Talent Acquisition process is building a Strategic Workforce Plan. This process is the only way to effectively blend strategy, talent requirements and accountability for results. It is what forms the basis of all effective recruiting and recruitment marketing.

Recruiting is an action-oriented, transaction-centric discipline. It is really easy to get lost in the ongoing flow of requirements and solutions. That's how you lose sight of the bigger issues.

A great workforce planning process makes sure that the entire Talent Acquisition team understands the market, the emerging skills, and the competitive landscape. Without a clear picture of these things, the positioning required by great employment branding and candidate experience generation is inevitably flawed.

With a clear picture of the market of skills and the specifics of talent evolution, job ads, descriptions, and their communication can be directly tailored to market realities. Knowing what you want, how the market is changing, and who is chasing you are the pillars of success in recruiting. It's how you make the end goal of workforce development come to life.

The B product integrates these three pillars of proactive Talent Acquisition into a single tool: Workforce Planning, Competitive Intelligence and Job Descriptions.

Using a model they call 'Talent Shaping', B organizes the current and future state of your workforce into an inventory of skills. Using a proprietary taxonomy (that expands the power of O-Net), B delivers a quantitative model of the future as a destination.

Along with the 'Talent Shape', B provides competitive intelligence on a job by job or skill by skill basis. This create the opportunity to understand and identify alternative sources of talent while watching the competition disclose its strategy.

Finally, the system includes the ability to understand and price job descriptions in alignment with the underlying supply and demand in the market. The Job Description builder lets you see what other companies call the skill you are chasing. It also helps you see new skills as they emerge.

B's vision of the future of Talent Acquisition is molecular, based in the assembly of skills. This perspective unleashes creative solutions that make it possible to move more quickly as an organization.

CERIDIAN

C's CEO, David Ossip earned his primary degree in Econometrics and was a TA in the topic for a few years. He is extremely active in the Toronto AI community. He is a Fellow at the Creative Destruction Lab at the University of Toronto, the heart of the AI community

As a result, his view (and his company's as well) is that the various predictive techniques and methods being applied in HR are never AI and rarely ML. The company sees its integrity being a critical issue in the naming and describing of their functionality. (If you've missed it, Toronto may well be the most important AI center on the planet.)

As a result, we almost missed their astonishing story. Of all of the companies we interviewed, Ceridian is the most focused on increasing the value of their offering. They think about this topic in incredible detail. The team's R&D is exclusively oriented to answer the question, 'How do we make our clients more effective by increasing the power and utility of our software suite?'

C takes the position that technology they haven't invented is not something they can take credit for. As a result, they do not champion their extensive use of state of the art open source tools and widely understood common predictive technologies. They simply use them to improve the quality of the customer's experience.

C plays down the technical hype while focusing on delivery. Their R&D processes include a continuous evaluation of ongoing learning and how to apply it to the customer's experience

The company was among the first to introduce automated coaching for relationship improvement as a part of its embedded services. It was the first step in a process designed to give users at all levels a range of options with which to address the current problem, It is difficult to express the degree to which this discipline is embedded in C's technical workforce

For example, client support is increasingly informed by predictive models that anticipate problems by comparing the current transaction flow with those that caused problems for other customers. That means C can issue an alert that warns a client of a problem before it happens. C is the only company that briefed this important approach. It runs continuously in the background as a quality check and a fail-safe system.

C audits their payroll processes in real time. That means taking the current run, comparing it to all that have come before and pointing out outliers and inconsistencies.

Historically, the implementation process involved giving the client an expansive and comprehensive spreadsheet to complete. It was long, involved and somewhat error prone. Today the firm makes a forecast of the required configuration details based on the other 3,000 plus customers and starts implementation for there.

The company is experimenting with voice capability that transcends any particular platform. As long as your tools (Alexa, Siri, Google) are registered with Dayforce, you will be able to carry on a conversation and complete transactions. As is the case for all players, the hurdle is figuring out inference.

Expect C to continue to raise the bar without being braggadocios.

CORNERSTONE ON DEMAND (C)

It's hard to overstate that advantages that come with having 31 Million users and 17 years' worth of data. While smaller players are starved for data to work with (and often have to take clients just to get data), companies like C have the problem of deciding where to invest their energy.

The company's goal is not to build a a standalone product for intelligence and analysis. Rather, they are focused on reducing the time users spend in the software while increasing the value that they get from that time.

For example, the system applies ML to predict what employees are at risk of not completing compliance training on time by leveraging a range of content, employee, and time-based factors. Furthermore, it is able to predict how administering courses differently or adjusting the course catalog based on these factors is likely to impact compliance rates across divisions and locations in the organization.

Another compliance oriented example: clients are able to identify compliance risk related to departments, individuals and courses. You can then drill down and discover factors that contribute to good/bad compliance, as well as simulate hypothetical changes to those factors and the impact those changes are predicted to have on the organization, ultimately saving money in regulatory fees.

C's approach harnesses what they know to make their clients more effective.

At a company gathering, I heard the CEO say that 'We call it AI in public and machine learning inside of the organization." That's an exact encapsulation of the difficulties companies have communicating about their efforts to embed intelligence in their software. The user base is looking for AI answers while there are few to give. It's easier to answer their questions than to try to educate at every step.

The risk in that approach is that when the hype turns, positioning as an AI provider will lead to sales friction. C is in a good place to handle the shift in the winds.

The challenge facing large enterprise providers is a lot like replacing the foundation in a house. You have to jack the house up, install the foundation and then lower the house on to it.

That's a good way of thinking about the task facing all of the major suite providers. In C's case, their historic product development process (lighting a thousand flames to see which ones burn) risks being a longer cycle. The interesting thing about C's business model is that it predictably produces winners. It just makes the strategy harder to articulate.

For that reason, we see C as being precisely equivalent to the other suite providers in their development process. They exemplify the challenge that buyers will face in the near future. Enterprise software houses will be known by their personas and the emphasis they place on the underlying set of disciplines. Mark C as the player who will make intelligent software be about optimizing organizational learning across the HR silos.

CROWDED (C)

C presents itself as a data refresh and matching tool for recruiting purposes. The idea is that companies are sitting on a vast pile of decaying data about candidates (people who applied for a job, maybe made it partway through selection or somehow ended up in the resume database). Crowded takes the old data and brings it up to date.

Coupled with the data refresh mechanism is a matching scheme that incorporates job posting history to customize the process. C uses historical job posting data to inform the matching process. The company's central value proposition is that historical data can be improved as an adjunct to current recruiting processes.

Simply, C updates old resume data base records while refining the matching process.

It would be a mistake to see them so simply.

As is the case in many areas of corporate data, the details about individuals are being collected by a wide variety of companies through a wide variety of means. From scraped social media sites to pure internet searches, there are a ton of companies building a supply and learning to sell it.

C acquires data from these companies rather than collecting it on their own. Their internal goal is to provide their customer with the best possible data at the time of a query. They have built a mechanism designed to buy the freshest, highest quality data at the lowest price possible at the time the data is needed.

The problem is tougher than it may seem at first.

In order to understand its data suppliers at the moment of a transaction, C must be able to continuously monitor the freshness, accuracy, and completeness of the data they supply. These variables change as the vendors acquire new sources or revise their business models.

Some suppliers are strong in one area and weak in another. C uses routine assessments to judge the current data quality of the suppliers. They acquire for the best deal at the moment.

This is a powerful construct that is broadly applicable. In every arena, the notion that there is a single source of truth is in decay. Most of the vendors in this study are building data sources that can supplement, improve, or disagree with existing data sources. A function like C uses to acquire data will be an essential market mechanism going forward.

ENGAGE TALENT (E)

There is an enclave of HR Technology companies near Charleston, SC. The unlikely tech hub is home to data centric HR firms. There is a growing data scientist community that serves the industry.

EngageTalent is a predictive sourcing tool. It will tell you the likelihood that a given candidate will respond to your job offer. It scores the likelihood that your outreach will be successful. It does three things: Candidate Research, Competitive Research and Market Research.

The company assembles a data stream of source material that covers the 90,000 American companies with more than 50 employees. That's 100 Million candidates and 30,000 sources of data. Each of the 100 Million candidates are scored on the likelihood that they want a new job.

That prediction is built on a model that covers the following weighted factors that increase an employee's desire to leave.

Company Data:
- M&A
- Leadership Changes
- Bankruptcy
- Restructure/Reorg/Cost Cutting
- Litigation/Scandals
- Data Breaches
- Reputation and Brand Image
- Underperformance
- Contract License/Loss

Employee Data:

- Supply and Demand
- Challenge/Progressions
- Tenure Milestones
- Life Milestones
- Peer Actions
- Education/Certification Milestones
- Location Specific Issues
- Industry Wide Issues

The relationship between and employee's industry, company and relative experience is surprisingly understudied. There are many things you can know about a person simply from their employer. For example, an examination of job postings can give you a clear picture of the company's technology stack. It's safe to assume that any employee will have experience with the relevant parts of that stack.
E parses job postings to acquire that intelligence. The data itself is browsable within the application. It is one of many data streams. EngageTalent means to create an inescapable research environment for corporate sourcers. It includes verified contact info.

    The company builds a model, scrapes the data, populates the data base, refreshes and learns along the way. Predicitive Analytics and a nest of data create an environment that actively supplements sourcer performance. It is intended to inform human performance rather than replace it.

GLINT (G)

Glint (G) calls itself the "People Success Platform." Using a combination of NLP and Machine Learning, the company helps executives stay on top of workforce sentiment. They call it 'visibility into employee engagement in real time."

At its core, G is a pulse survey tool that promises "visibility, insight and action.' A standard set of survey questions drive feedback about well-accepted engagement factors. Companies may add their own tailoring.

G uses NLP to process open-ended text responses to the various polls it creates. By coupling a taxonomy (built around engagement factors) with sentiment analysis, G offers a richer, synthetic view of workforce health. According to their literature, '... Narrative Intelligence connects the dots between what your employees say, how they feel, and the relationship to engagement and other outcomes.'

Immediately following the completion of a survey, G creates recommended action plans for each manager in the company. Based on feedback from their team, managers are offered a range of suggestions, prioritized for potential impact. For each prioritized area, G offers a tutorial library of suggested changes.

In this way, G resembles the original game plan for Success Factors. In its earliest incarnations, Success Factors was a set of best practices and a tool for understanding how and when to apply them. It was a managerial improvement coach in a box. G conforms to that approach.

The package tracks improvement plans and measures their results.

To get started, the system requires access to the client's HRIS. Performance management, outcome measures and adjacent survey data may be included for added insight. While G did not mention this in demos, there must be a reasonable relationship to data quantity and quality and initial effectiveness. We would expect a subset of customers to encounter the need for remedial data work.

The service includes extensive training of end users, ongoing evaluation of results (interpretation and recommendations) and executive coaching. G, like many of the companies in this survey, sees their service as a point of departure for a conversation rather than an end in itself.

One might see G as a freestanding version of the toolkit UltimateSoftware is embedding in its platform. The market development challenge involves the rate at which transparency and machine generated management recommendations become the norm.

Overall, G is an important indicator of the degree to which employee feedback is becoming a navigational tool for company leaders.

HIREMYA (M)

M is the most advanced and broadly deployed of the chatbot segment.

That's partly because the niche and the system requirements are simple and easy to execute. By focusing on very simple, low level hourly jobs, M is able to generate proof of concept evidence that suggests that larger things are possible. None of the competition takes this approach. That leaves M with key, large scale customers, great investors and a record of success.

They recently signed a three-year deal (following a 12-month trial period) with Adecco. That is the perfect customer for this hourly focused, text based recruiting 'assistant'.

Hourly recruiting in the light industrial sector is boring. A large part of the problem is that human recruiters are slow to follow uo on received applications. Because churn is fast, pay is low and workers can't afford to wait around, a lot of recruiting operations have miserable close rates. By instantly following up on an application and scheduling the interview, Mya takes much of the friction out of the process.

Hiring hourly laborers with text messaging through their cell phones is a straightforward proposition. Requirements are limited and speed is always the essence of the deal. The same is true of retail and some call centers.

The tool works because the decision tree is simple. The results are pretty amazing. They reduce the applicant to hire ratio from 10 to 1 to 4 to one. This dramatically decreases the recruiting workload. The secret is simple. A rapid timely response always trumps a longer cycle time.

The other metric of interest is that the tool increases the 'connect rate' from 34% to 91%. That's the rate at which applicants are contacted and a live person is on the other end of the deal. Again, the impact of speed cannot be overstated.

The next frontiers for M include the automation of sourcing, refreshing contact data, regular outreach with text to build the talent pool.

It's often the case that the simplest solutions are the most successful. That's true in this case.

HIRETUAL (H)

You pronounce the company's name one of two ways: Hire-tool or Hire-to-el. The second is the intended form. It's the combination of hire and virtual.

The team of 10 is housed in San Jose, CA. For staffing purposes, they blend data scientists, developers and recruiters. Founder Steven Jiang is particularly proud of the depth of recruiting expertise within the company's walls. Co-founder Ninh Tran is a former Googler and angel investor

Jiang frames the company as an operation with a mission - to become the recruiter's best friend. That mission drives them to have a vision of a logarithmic improvement in sourcing and/or hiring from using 'intelligence technology.'

With 'several hundred' customers, the company is a grassroots favorite in the Recruiting community with a number of well-known advisors and advocates.

On the simplest level, H does three things

- It takes a job description and turns it into a comprehensive Boolean search string;
- It finds contact information for candidates; and,
- If you feed it a job description, it will return a ranked short list of candidates.

The tool is developed using open source tools for data mining and deep learning. Essentially, the company aggregates data from two sources: partnerships with commercial data providers and data scraped from around the web. Like others, they build profiles of individuals and claim to have the largest library of contact information 'on the web.' Like most companies claiming AI, there is little to support the notion.

The system learns the nuances of a customer's needs and preferences over time. According to Jiang, "training data gets us to 70% effectiveness. The rest is learned from client utilization." In his view, it takes about a month for the tool to start to deliver results that reflect a clear difference from the initial data set.

All companies experience pivots, redirections, cost cutting and other shifts that rearrange the recruiting teams priorities. Jiang believes that it would take 'a couple of months' to recover from that experience. The firm has not had a customer that underwent that sort of transition just yet.

Implementation is a 24 hour process. The company spins up a new instance and the customer begins using the tool.

H is typical of first generation machine led intelligence. It automates, with a layer of extra intelligence, current processes. They are focused there, on contemporary recruiter performance.

HIREVUE (HV)

Founded in 2004, HV began its life with a focus on video interviewing. The company began to earnestly pursue an expanded vision about five years ago. The idea is that video interviewing is both a communications vehicle and an astonishing data source. By sampling facial expressions every half second, the company can accumulate 25,000 data points in a fifteen-minute interview.

The company assembled an impressive team of data scientists and I/O psychologists who have taken those data points and correlated them with historically proven assessment science. The result is an emerging set of tools that can predict, with meaningful accuracy, who will fit and who will fail. HV is assembling other tools (like the capability to test and evaluate coding skills) that use smart software and statistics to reduce friction and improve effectiveness in the recruiting process. They have one of the most interesting R&D functions in the report.

They combine interviewing, assessment and prescreening into a single predictive process for bulk hiring. To be fair, they claim that they can overcome small scale hiring problems by using data from across companies

The approach is somewhat controversial. While the underlying science is proven, there's an 'ickiness' associated with imagining that your facial tics are being used to evaluate your personality (the tool doesn't actually do this). The science of measuring physical attributes to determine cultural fitness has a bad history in the past several centuries. HireVue assures me that they only evaluate 'microexpressions'. It's a difficult claim to evaluate.

Still, the intrusion of various sensors into our lives is part and parcel of the emerging technology. Although it remains unclear how privacy regulations will evolve, this sort of measurement is unlikely to be abandoned. HireVue is a pioneer.

As this particular strain of technology continues to evolve, it will be increasingly difficult to distinguish recruiting from job trials. As a result, the underlying skillset of recruiters will grow to include a more quantitative assessment of potential as well as a deeper reading of what it means to be able to do the job. When the workflow is compressed and improved, the human decision makers will have to improve and focus their game.

There did not appear to be a way to argue with the recommendations that the system makes. HV's claim to offer 'recommendations only with decision making left to the humans' is more than a little fanciful. It is unclear how a human decision maker would be able to justify making an alternative decision. As long as the machine has the data and makes a numeric evaluation, the decisions are pretty well cooked.

This is where HV's team excels. They are very clear that their tool is used most effectively in volume hiring. They say that the real place for human decision making that is at odds with their output is in the mid-range. The top candidates are the top candidates. Which of the 70 percenters you want to choose is where the human decision making really resides.

A final note. Because video interviewing always carries a question about implicit bias (does seeing the candidate bias the recruiting decision), HV is building a reputation for expertise in the statistical understanding and management of systemic bias.

HUMANYZE (H)

H is different from all of the other companies evaluated in this research. **Co-founded by Ben Waber, Daniel Olguin, Taemie Kim, and Tuomas Jaanu, researchers** with fundamental ties to MIT's famous Media Lab, the company focuses on organizational measurement. Where all of the other companies in this research think about organizations as a collection of individuals, H views the organization itself as the fundamental element of inquiry.

A badge that contains a microphone, Bluetooth and an accelerometer are used to track location and interactions. A digital communications system monitors flow and metadata of non-physical channels. The combination is displayed as a social network analysis.

This creates a near real-time picture of how work actually happens and the actual social dimensions of people inside the organization. The team at H make it easy to understand why traditional views of HR problems that address the individual without regard to their role fail so often. Culture-fit, personality assessment, skills analysis, and other matching paradigms fall short because the actual 'job' exists in a specific social construct. H makes that visible.

For example, with a good real-time network map, you can experiment with and quickly see the results of rearranging the operation to optimize workflow. Waber once told me that 'The position of the coffee pot matters way more than the diagrams on the org chart." H allows you to test the coffee pot hypothesis by moving it around and then measuring what happens.

H is top of mind for people in operations, manufacturing and finance. While HR tends to be focused on administration workflows, the rest of the business is deadly serious about making money. When shifting the organization around can generate higher productivity and profitability, the people with P?L responsibility move quickly.

That means that H is a part of a bow wave of transformation coming to the traditional HR disciplines. When people science has direct bottom line impact, it's easy to get operating management to sign up. That's why H's customer base is skewed away from HT.

If there were one technology we'd suggest HR understand, this is it.

Somewhat surprisingly, H makes no claims about AI, digital technology or recommendations for decisions. Rather, it is focused on getting as clear a picture as possible of what actually happens. With that in hand, management can make powerful decisions on their own.

If you think about it long enough, you'd have questions about the privacy implications of H's approach. They have the most thorough approach to securing privacy that I've encountered.

H demonstrates how to apply advanced technology to HR problem sets without resorting to hype or increasing customer liability.

I's predictive tools coalesce around what once was the Kenexa organization. Acquired in 2012, Kenexa was itself an amalgam of earlier organization. The demo featured an updated version of BrassRing and some references to Salary.com (which was acquired by I and then resold to its founders).

While the heart of I's branding claims involve the company's branded brain, the execution details are all about improving the speed and quality of recruiting transactions.

The tools covered in the demo:

- **Improved Talent Attraction and Acquisition**
  Tools to increase recruiter efficiency and candidate quality
- **Augmented Talent Engagement and Development**
  Beginning with 'social listening'. IBM refers to the area as 'Cognitive Talent Management.'

Rather than focusing on strategy, the tool seeks to improve Recruiter productivity by continuously prioritizing the workload. I defines 'priority' as a combination of process completion and recruiting requisition complexity. It looks at the recruiter's workload and delivers a rank ordered set of tasks based on measures that are likely to result in a more optimal performance.

It's really a form of management by machine that identifies potential workflow bottlenecks and plows through them. In each task, the recruiter can see the drivers of the complexity and process completion scores. The system takes recruiter feedback about its recommendations in a comment form. The system also monitors actual recruiter behavior and learns from that as well.

I also ranks candidates on the measures it determines to be the five most important. The recruiter is presented with a ranked and sorted list with the highest-ranking candidates at the top. Again, the system takes feedback and learns from recruiter performance.

The early versions of Talent Engagement tools begin with 'social listening', a tool that summarizes the various reviews a company receives.

The most intelligent of the offerings is a smart chatbot called Myca. The animated search interface 'learns' about candidates and builds a 'relationship' with them. Myca presents candidates with jobs for which they are qualified but may not have sought. The same functionality is used to drive internal career management processes.

JOBERATE (J)

Companies like J are possible because of the combination of open source tools for data science/predictive modeling and the Minimum Viable Product (MVP) development strategy. A healthy growing ecosystem of tools slashes initial development costs. MVP allows new companies to partner with their clients in the development process.

J scores the likelihood that an individual will change jobs.

CEO Michael candidly observes that he is learning about his product every day by working with and listening to clients. All customers get access to Morpheus, the company's database of enhanced profiles built from data in social media. The company's search results are intentionally skewed to create a bias towards the hiring of protected classes according to Beygelman.

This part of the product is structurally similar to TalentBin, Monster's 'scraped' database pf candidate data. It is central to what Beygleman calls 'identity resolution' (the ability to clearly differentiate people with the same name).

The interesting thing about the J approach is that under these circumstances, customers invent pretty interesting use cases.

Each profile is scored for the likelihood that the individual will change jobs. There is a numeric score and a color-coded range (red, yellow, green). The scoring system involves a deep investigation of social media behavior. Patterns of follows, tweets, bio changes and other seemingly insignificant transactions show deep significance as predictors of job change behavior.

With a reported 330 Million profiles under management, the company is focused on two things:

- Enhancing the reliability and validity of its predictions, and
- Refining its two basic use cases – retention and recruiting

- **Retention**
    - One large customer tracks real time job hunting behavior of all employees
    - Another very large customer tracks the correlation between job hunting behavior and corporate announcements.
- **Recruiting**
    - Build talent pools of people you want to headhunt
    - Compare classes of employees to the same class of employee in a competitor
    - Measure of employer of choice by comparing attrition rates
    - Evaluate attrition likelihood by supervisor in a large workforce

J is a controversial vendor who, with HiQ labs (not evaluated in this report) are attempting to integrate internal data with flight risk calculations. The approach has deployment issues as noted in the report.

JOYOUS (J)

J is the brainchild of Michael Carden, founder and CEO. Carden is the New Zealander entrepreneur whose Sonar6 introduced new age performance management to the HRTech industry. The company eventually sold to Cornerstone.

With deep industry familiarity, clear lines of personal funding, a satisfied client network, and a leg up on industry visibility, we're covering J at an earlier stage than any other company in the survey. They have a better change of surviving and prospering as a result of Carden's inputs and investment.

J is rooted in the notion that all forms of feedback, from pulse and engagement surveys to performance management are a part of a continuous flow of information between employer and employee as well as among employees. Transparency requires being able to see and understand the entirety of the flow. The tool integrates surveys, 360-feedback, performance management and their synthesis/rollup at management levels.

J delivers all employee processes through the same beautiful user interface, on a day to day basis. It is envisioned as a more sophisticated messaging system that is coupled with sentiment analysis and machine learning to deeply discover the underlying truths about the company and its employees.

Carden believes that the single largest problem in HRTech is the proliferation of User Interfaces. By making communications hard and requiring multiple ways of delivering the same message, HR systems themselves are at the heart of HR's biggest problems. Carden imagines a coming reduction in the number of UIs.

J asks its prospects to engage in a thought experiment: "Instead of asking dozens of questions and hoping that you land on the truth, why not ask simple questions on a weekly basis? How was your day? What's it like to work for Sammy? Is the company honest? What do you think of the product?

And, then letting machine learning and NLP mine the output for underlying themes.

Carden is deeply involved in coding and testing J. He says that some of the biggest investments they've made are in the development of software to produce usable fake data. That's because testing the product has a catch. You can't test without data and you can't get data without customers. So, you have to create your own.

With J deployed in the organization as the primary communications tool for organization feedback and performance management, it becomes possible to directly see the ties between engagement and performance. The tool uses intelligent technology to distill insight from the volumes of input.

Carden is fond of saying that we are still looking for the same needles in the haystack. There's just a ton more hay.

KAREN.AI (Karen)

The company is an 8-month-old, early stage operation. They are rapidly building momentum with a series of large scale enterprise wins. "Karen" is billed as 'your cognitive Recruiting assistant."

Chatbot technology is notoriously difficult to get right. With a fair number of offerings that claim comprehensive utility, karen.ai (Karen) stands out for its commitment to a very specific focus.

Karen is designed to:

- Review resumes, hundreds per second, and highlight quality candidates;
- Engage candidates in text or SMS
- Reduce human interviewing time. (This is really a benefit of the first two processes.)

Like many tools that feature Machine Learning, Karen works best on volume problems. The company sees its sweet spot as jobs where 25 or more hires are made each year. Less than that and there are too few transactions from which to learn.

Karen combines NLP and ML into a single black box. Resumes are deconstructed using NLP techniques. Then, the system learns which resumes meet the criterial. The feedback between the two techniques enables Karen to become increasingly sophisticated in its attempts to create shortlists.

The company is headquartered in Toronto, Ontario, Canada. The area is rapidly becoming the most important hub for AI technology on the North American continent.

Like many of the projects in this report, Karen is building an NLP translation system (a taxonomy) that allows the system to understand the relationship between key variables. The core hurdle in NLP projects is always teaching the machine to understand differences and similarities in the turn of a phrase.

The tool builds on data about company culture, job descriptions, a personality inventory and the aforementioned taxonomy to discover quality matches.

The pilot experimentation process involves a mechanical process of

- A human review of 1,000 resumes
- A review of the human results with detailed investigation of the reasons for accepting or rejecting a resume;
- A joint human machine review of 1,000 resumes; and,
- A machine review of 1,000 resumes.

The machine's results are validated and become the starting point for future recommendations.

The company's culture is hyper-sensitive to the impact of AI on the livelihoods of professional recruiters. This was a distinguishing element of our demo.

The team has been involved in several of the AI community building and education initiatives from both the NextAI and the IBM Global Entrepreneur Program.

"We've gotten really good at designing custom algorithms," says co-founder Josh Jarrett. "There's a world of variation for the same job between organizations. An investment banker at Morgan Stanley is unlike someone with the same job at Goldman."

K uses a set of well-defined soft skills (the Koru7™Impact Skills: Grit, Rigor, Impact, Teamwork, Curiosity, Ownership and Polish) as the foundation for a measure of cultural fit. Each customer's complete algorithm is tailored from there.

K thinks of this as 'competency based hiring. The process starts with a 20 minute pre-interview (it's an instrument, a survey). The idea is that each company culture requires a particular constellation of soft skills as the foundation of success in the job.

K positions itself as a skills measure. This allows them to claim that they are not a personality assessment, better than a cognitive assessment, and different from technical skills evaluations. (On an important side note, K claims that technical skills are not the primary drivers' of job success.)

With K, candidates are screened in based on predictive factors ('what they can do')

The K 'fingerprint' is a subset of the 250 variables that the company evaluates through a combination of big data and assessment science. Underneath it all is a rigorous dedication to scientific validity.

The founding team is a high-powered pair of senior players from the Microsoft-Gates Foundation Universe. With history at McKinsey and in the Learning segments of both Gates founded operations, they come to the HRTech/Recruiting scene full of optimism and people science.

Historically, assessment oriented companies have limited success in recruiting. There are multiple factors involved. There are very few long-term career recruiters. Most people enter and leave the profession in a couple of years. In addition, assessment oriented utilities have significant up-front investments required from both sides: the tool set must be customized and candidates must take an instrument.

These are the bits of friction that sow the adoption of really smart technologies. And, they are the uphill battle faced by companies like K. eHarmony's failure in the space is a cautionary tale. The science was right, the technique was okay but the resistance to measurement was severe.

If anyone can cross this threshold, K can. They've built the right team and work diligently to reduce the friction. They are the best in the current class of predictive performance assessment competitors.

KRONOS (K)

K is 40 years old. It began life with the simple idea that time keeping (time cards) could be easier. The company patented the first microprocessor based time clock. In the intervening years, the company has innovated and acquired its way to a client base of more than 30,000. Revenue was about $1.5B in the year ending June 30, 2017. The company has 3,400 direct employees.

This is a big company that straddles a broad range of industries. It delivers a full spectrum of HR services. It's focus, relatively obviously, is the hourly workforce that utilizes its time and attendance products. You might imagine that the company sees itself as doing 'age appropriate' things. It behaves exactly like a powerful billion-and-a-half-dollar company that is focused on perfecting its execution.

K sees predictive tools as a part of their ongoing efforts to deliver insight and utility in their reporting services. It's an interesting way of looking at the potential of the technology that is very consonant with their roots. Imagine trying to teach 30,000 existing customers how to think about the utility of predictions.

That means that the K initiatives involving intelligent tech are focused on specific pain points that their customers face each day.

Take transforming timecard data into project info and comparing it to a project plan and schedule. That requires K to acquire a data feed from SAP and reformat their data (mapping plus allocation splits) to the hierarchical framework in the SAP data. This time-consuming process can be easily executed with intelligent software that is able to sense structural differences in the SAP flow.

K routinely expands and transforms the data models provided by enterprise companies (not just SAP but Oracle, Workday, Infor).

Other functions include developing 'landing estimates'. Based on history and accounting for current conditions, the time keeping system can predict total labor consumption for the week based on Monday's consumption. The system then offers multiple paths to finishing the week at the agreed upon budget.

As a part of the introduction of intelligent tools, K touts full time access to 'persisted data' as a key feature. Historically (for all vendors), data storage was an expensive part of any contract. Snapshots of data were archived instead of a robust copy of everything ever. Today's products are better able to be harnessed for ML because a comprehensive data set is available. This feels like a point of differentiation that would really matter to older clients with legacy outlooks.

Like the best players in the business, Kronos begins with its strengths and focuses on imagining new functionality to improve its customers effectiveness.

LEAP.AI (L)

L is a machine-learning project that focuses on improving the skills and culture match between resumes and jobs. The company currently spends all of its energy on a small subset of the high-tech sector. It has significant traction there because its founders have deep roots in the Google machine learning community.

L sees its target market as fast growth (pre IPO) companies with 200 or more employees. This is a common configuration in industries where Venture Capital firms invest in R&D. With investment, growth is unconstrained by available revenue. In other words, Leap.ai positions itself as a specialty tool focused on reducing recruiting errors when companies try to achieve rapid scale.

With a combination of client interviews and hiring history, L seeks to identify the things that make the culture of one company different from the other. It's a practical problem to solve with 200 employees and significantly harder when there are 10,000 or more. L seems to be pointing to some interesting structural ideas about culture; that matching is more complex the larger the company.

The company's customers include Uber, Lyft, Evernote, Zoom, Cloudera and another 25 or so fast-moving Silicon Valley startups. There are 15 full time employees and 8 interns currently at work at the company. Richard Liu, one of the founding engineers, described the company as "...focused on the development of infrastructure. You cannot build a really big company by focusing on tool development, you have to be able to handle the transaction and processing load that comes with scale."

Liu founded the company because "I have hired hundreds of people at Google and found the experience unsatisfactory for everyone involved."

When Liu talks about infrastructure, he means that he is laying the groundwork for a wholly owned data center. Where most of the competitors in this arena are using amazon, Google or one of the other storage and processing services, there is a move towards independence that is led by Dropbox. Uninterrupted service with no significant bottlenecks is the long-range goal. Leap.ai will be an interesting test point to see if this assertion matters in HRTech.

The high-tech industry is small with roughly 8 million workers. The subset of those that work in rapid growth venture backed startups is a minor percentage. L will have to expand beyond its comfort zone in order to remain viable. This did not seem to be a part of their game plan.

The hiring universe is complex. Culture ebbs and flows as companies grow. The fit between an individual and a company remains elusive and may not be best represented by hiring history. The company could use an infusion of industry awareness and expertise.

PHENOM PEOPLE

PhenomPeople is a tool that manages traffic acquisition, job matching and initial selection through a company's employment website. It delivers a customized experience for the job hunter that improves with each visit. The company has real traction with large scale customers like Microsoft, Philips, General Motors and Citrix.

The product delivers tailored content and job feeds to employment website visitors based on a profile built from interactions and the visitor's resume. The idea is that the increasingly personalized experience will provide a better candidate experience. As the experience gets better, the visitor is increasingly likely to return.

The team expects that their tool will be useful for referral programs, internal mobility, career site operations, university recruiting, alumni relations, building 'talent communities', and, the management of career related events.

The individual talent profile is a combination of aggregated social media information, online behavior, and internal company data (from the ATS and the HRIS).

PP describes its development efforts as 'building four graphs:
- A Candidate Graph
- A Jobs Graph
- A Recruiter/Hiring Manager Graph
- An Employee Graph.

In addition, the tool automatically classifies a new job. Based on the classification, it develops and executes an online advertising strategy to drive candidate traffic.

Overtime, PP aspires to build a universal set of descriptors for jobs, web visitors and organizations. The objective of this work is to be able to readily predict successful fit while removing friction from the labor market.

In a somewhat contradictory thread, PP described a deep commitment to a future without web traffic. "We imagine a world with 30% less web traffic within three to five years." As a result, PP is focusing future development on chatbots and voice based interfaces.

The company's strong market traction comes, in part, from its ties to the Candidate Experience movement. Ed Newman, the company's chief evangelist, is one of the founders of the Candidate Experience Awards and a long-time veteran of the industry. His involvement, coupled with PPs deep technology bench make it likely that this is one of the winners.

PYMETRICS (P)

P wants to be the most widely used predictive tool for career matching. That puts them in the position of straddling adjacent but different markets in HR, Advertising and Education. For the most part, career oriented activities are a part of the education system. While HR may spend some energy on Career oriented activities, it's usually a part of a retention process and not really very employee centric. The Advertising market (job boards and other career enhancing services) rarely are connected enough to the actual opportunity to offer much in the way of insight.

So, while the ambition is honorable, it is flawed in the way that new entrants to the HRTech/Recruiting market often misunderstand things. There simply are no altruistic players with budget to spend on improved career satisfaction for individuals. That group only exists in the education market and only as an expression of university marketing.

P has 30 employees and 25 customers. The offices are in the startup sector of Manhattan. They use ML techniques to help companies understand the drivers of employee success within the culture. This is the classic definition of an assessment company. The Pymetrics difference is gamification.

The assessment process involves using:
- Individual employee data
- Performance management/goal achievement data
- The measured relevance of 70 separate traits.
- Gamification tackles the 70 discrete traits.

They use neurocognitive tools that measure both cognitive and emotional traits. It's worth noting that direct competitors claim that there is no predictive relevance of cognitive/emotional traits.

Of all of the companies evaluated in this research, P had the most structured understanding of the regulatory climate. They design their processes to meet the EEOC's 4/5 rule of thumb. That is, a process is generally not discriminatory of the members of a minority class pass a given workflow hurdle at a rate of at least 80% of the majority class.

In all, P is a fantastic product of well-disciplined science. The question of product-market fit is a different thing. They are well worth watching.

SALARY.COM (S)

S is an amazing entrepreneurial story. Founded by CEO Kent Plunkett in the late 1990s, the company went public, was sold to IBM and repurchased by the original team. Throughout the journey, the product set new benchmarks for the improvement of salary visibility.

Early on, Plunkett and his team recognized that the business of keeping compensation data timely was the future. In those days, there were no internet sources. Large compensation consulting firms conducted small comp surveys and then sold the results. Participants were given a discount.

When S came to the market, it was the first time that an employee could acquire real-time data to bring to a salary discussion. The model treated the market as a two-sided conversation and S serviced both sides of the conversation.

As a result, they became aware of the dynamic nature of the job market through direct experience. It wasn't simply salary data that changed rapidly, it was all of the underlying support information in competencies, job descriptions and taxonomies. The company learned to automate the evolution of the myriad working parts of the compensation information infrastructure.

The underlying database and its structure evolve at the speed of the labor market, prompted by individual client queries to the system. It's as if the massive database of job titles, regional variations, industry specifics and skills evolution were tended by automated landscapers. In order to deliver timely, accurate and relevant information, the company pioneered the use of ML in HR Data.

One of the key elements of this application is its taxonomy (the organizing structure for the data). It turns out that enterprise systems rarely come with one. By adding a unique job and information architecture to an ERP platform, the HR data begins to expand in utility. With algorithms and machine leraning, S is delivering new and dynamic ways to match jobs and determine pay with highly visual data and predictive analytics.

Like the platform providers, S doesn't flash its technical expertise. It prefers to deliver extraordinary customer experience without spending a lot of time explaining the underlying mechanics. The company recently released a complete product rewrite designed to multiply customer value while reducing the time required to use the system.

Compensation decisions involve market sensibilities that are hard to automate. S helps clients tee up compensation decisions without dictating the answer. It avoids the problem of confusing users with recommendations that feel like directions. Instead, the company includes heuman technical support for individual job pricing as well as systemic issues.

S represents the epitome of baked in technology. They use the latest intelligent tools to build systems that increase a client's effectiveness.

SCOUT (S)

S is an example of the kinds of revolutionary structures that are becoming possible. In recruiting, many companies utilize the services of third party firms to fill specific staffing needs. Often, the area is handled by purchasing rather than HR. The resulting scramble of responsibilities makes it hard to manage in either procurement or HR.

S delivers a combination of crowd sourcing and marketplace that allows a company to control- its contingent search spend and results in a way that simply wasn't possible before. Employers publish job descriptions to the marketplace. Recruiters compete for the work. The company gets one invoice for all of the recruiting.

S is paid with a percentage of the cashflow. The employer gets standardization of services and consolidated accounting. The recruiter gets broader horizons in business development.

At the core the Employer-to-Search Firm Recruiter Performance Matching is its Machine-Learning Based Recommendation Engine. The Engine uses NLP to understand the unstructured text of jobs posted to the marketplace. Next, S generates dense vector representations of job titles and descriptions.

S engineers model recruiter history in terms of these job vectors, as well as user's geographical preferences and previous company relationships. Next, regression analysis is applied to score the suitability of each job to each recruiter (or employer to search firm recruiter) which serves as the basis for the recommendations. In the future, S plans to apply similar machine learning tools to curate and rank candidates.

S is a fantastic example of how to use emerging technology to reduce workloads, increase value and simplify intractable problems.

SMARTRECRUITERS (SR)

SmartRecruiters is a San Francisco based Recruiting Software startup. They have received $54.96M in 4 Rounds from 7 High Quality Investors. Company founder, Jerome Ternynck is an entrepreneur who founded and sold Mr. Ted, the ATS at the heart of Lumesse.

The SR data science department was built by the team at JobSpotting, a Berlin operation staffed with former members of the Google search team. SmartRecruiters purchased and integrated Jobspotting in January 2017.

The combination of market savvy and subject matter expertise makes the SR team a potential industry powerhouse. They view their job market intelligence operation as a recommendation engine. The goal is to remove friction from the recruiting process while improving the quality of the candidate's experience. The Berlin based engineering team focuses on three areas:

- Classification
    - Classifying resumes
    - Scoring candidates based on their relevance to the company and the job
- Automation
    - Basic tasks (reviewing and sorting resumes, making short lists)
    - Enriching resumes with data from the internet (capsule information about the companies mentioned in the resume, for example)
- Recommendation
    - Recruitment marketing (programmatic to candidates and the open market)
    - Quickly finding similar people for the same job or similar jobs for the same person

Jobspotting founder, Hessam Lavi, says, "We spend about 80% of our time canonicalizing data in order to make our models more effective." Canonicalization is the process of taking disparate data and making them sortable or intelligible in some other standardized fashion. Building coherent models of job related data requires massive attention to canonicalization.

"We are organized as an engineering problem solving team," says Lavi. We use whatever tools are appropriate to solve the challenge at hand. It's better to imagine us as a workshop with the best tools than as a single problem-solving method." That means that the team thinks very carefully about the issues surrounding categorization, matching, searching and forecasting.

Unlike most of the other players, SR does not automatically improve its process with learning and feedback. They put a delay in the process between learning and a change in the training data. This allows them to minimize and control the introduction of bias into decision making.

"We build smart agents that help Recruiters make better decisions. Humans will never be replaced in this process because there is no ultimate source of truth. Recruiting will always depend on human insight. We just improve it."

At the stand alone ATS level, there is no better intelligent augmentation of a software product.

SWOOP TALENT (ST)

There are two critical problems faced by most owners of Human Resource Information Systems (HRIS). The data is always incomplete, usually by significant proportions. To complicate matters worse, what data there is comes in a variety of formats. Incompleteness is multiplied by lack of interconnection.

While there are other significant data quality issues in any HR data implementation, incompleteness and disconnectedness are the primary problems in using the HRIS as a foundational part of a machine led decision making system. The ST service cleans data, merges disparate data sources, discovers new information and improves discovery. It is primarily used to enhance data in the HRIS.

There are other bits of functionality that relate to the company's origins as a sourcing tool.

ST uses vector modeling to inventory and index the client's data archives.

Vector Modeling is based on the premise that any collection of text can be reduced to a mathematical formula. There can be many different formulas attributed to a body of text depending on the emphasis of the equation writer. For example, the formula that describes a novel could be designed to count the number of occurrences of a prioritized list of words. That would be a different formula than one created with no list of words.

The technique can be used for matching purposes (find all of the documents with the following sets of words) or for aligning two sets of data without a pivot field (find the relative commonalities between the columns in these two sets of data).

In short, ST is perfecting the use of the Vector Model in an HR context. While the technique is being used to accomplish other things in HRTech, no one else is solving this specific problem set.

TALENT SONAR (TS)

It would be easy to confuse TalentSonar (TS) with some of the other startups that focus on the intersection of culture, skills and recruiting. The founders of machine led decision making HR Startups rarely come from the HR Technology industry. For the most part, they are engineers and computer science with a good working theory about HR or Recruiting.

This is not a new phenomenon. Computer scientists rarely take on HR as a profession. It is even rarer that HR practitioners become software developers or product managers.

That makes it easy to handicap the success chances of small startups. What matters is how curious the principals are about the industry and its unique nuances. The history of venture backed HR Technology failure is littered with stories of entrepreneurs with revolutionary ideas who never bothered to study the problem they proposed to solve.

TS is a San Francisco based startup founded by Laura Mather, a seasoned entrepreneur whose history includes large scale security oriented technologies. The company is using predictive analytics as a part of its workbench. The company's mission is to expand the candidate pool to previously untapped and under-represented groups and ensure the best person is hired for the job, regardless of race, gender, school, or any other criterion that isn't relevant to how well the person will perform in the job.

The company offers an array of tools designed to ensure hiring decisions are made based on relevant criteria. **Ensuring hiring teams are successful in their goal of adding skill, experience and perspective** means keeping the hiring process focused on merit. They include:

- Prioritized Job Skill Sets
- Inclusive Job Descriptions
- Blind Resume Review

- Structured Interviews

TS uses a range of intelligent technologies to solve the following specific problems:

- **Inclusive Job Descriptions**

    This function is similar to textio, who examine job descriptions for hot words that indicate cultural barriers. TS is particularly looking to increase the volume of hiring in African American and Latino sub-categories. They have no plans to venture away from this very specific set of targets.

- **Resume Redaction**

    TS believe that it is necessary to redact all personal identifying information (no matter how slight) from a resume. This ensures an evaluation on the merits rather than from the connection that comes from identification. They are able to remove identifiable traces from 92 out of 100 resumes. As they learn, the success rate will climb.

TS does not try to reduce the number of resumes in the funnel. Rather it uses self-improving algorithms to keep job descriptions inclusive, uses predictive analytics to remove where names and other identifying information occur in resumes. The job description language changes over time but continuously reflects the attributes of the dominant majority.

TALLA (T)

According to Talla's (T) CEO, Rob May, soon you will be able to visit the company's website and hire a digital worker. T builds chatbots for IT and HR currently. Of all of the entrepreneurs we've talked with, May is the most upfront about the fact that the technology is uncertain.

May is sober in his reflection and ambition. That's exactly what you want from the management of a company that plans to provide you with digital employees. A clear understanding of the risks and benefits of digital intelligence is a necessary component of decision making.

He says that he is trying to build the world's best business paraphrasing system. The description reflects

May's realism distinguishes him from many of the other purveyors of chatbot technology. He would rather set a realistic set of expectations and build a relationship than promise the moon.

Currently, T works in slack, Microsoft Teams, ServiceNow, JIRA, and Gmail. It uses a combination of NLP and Machine Learning to cobble together a core level of intelligence. May estimates that threshold to be somewhere between 50% and 65%. It takes about 2 months for the new digital employee to get that good at her work.

From there, the work is about building the underlying database one query at a time. As the tool seeks to learn meaning and intent, a queue of misunderstood queries is developed for human processing and adjustment. It's a very incremental process that assumes a team of trainers with no malicious intent.

(I know that I'd be tempted, from time to time, to teach the Chatbot some stupid tricks and bad answers. I have to assume that I'm not alone in having a slightly malicious sense of humor.)

There are three models for NLP:

- Parse and Understand. Generates a 40% success rate.

- Sequence to sequence (works best in academia b/c requires large data sets)
- Sentence similarity (this is what T is currently utilizing)

If you are going to invest in adding machine led decision making to your arsenal, the single most important factor in the decision is your appraisal of the supplier's integrity. Talla is the top of that list. May was very explicit about the technical challenges he is facing. Understanding the intent of one set of questions is taking many times more investment and energy than predicted in the plan.

Introducing intelligence into your organization is no small thing. Like any new employee in need of training and coaching, the up front costs of ownership are still hard to pin down. This applies to all of the tools in this report.

That said, T is a good bet as a starting point for experimentation with digital employees. T sees them that way.

TEXTIO (T)

T owns the most beautiful and effective interface design of any company in this evaluation. Jensen Harris, the company's Co-founder and CTO is a powerhouse designer with credits that cover many of Microsoft's flagship products. Elegant and focused, the interfaces goal is to "make simple the massive amount of data and analysis under the hood."

The company's vision transcends its origins in HR/Recruiting: "...the future of writing is knowing how well your words will work before anyone else reads them. To power this revolution, we are building a remarkable augmented writing platform that people are falling in love with. We are—quite literally—changing the way people write."

In its current incarnation, T is designed to improve the effectiveness of job postings. A user uploads a job ad and the tool scores it. T's data shows that the more gender neutral a job description is, the faster it will fill. Gender neutral job descriptions fill 14 days faster on average.

The underlying data set includes 250 million job postings collected at the rate of 10 million/month. The company uses the database to test effectiveness in a variety of settings. They score and evaluate over 60,000 companies on job posting effectiveness in the textio index.

The offering uses a combination of NLP, ML and customer data to understand the impact of individual word on fill rates, application volume and the gender mix of applicants. There is a dynamic, real time interaction between editorial changes. The user is guided through an editing process in which the score improves with each relevant change. There is an instantaneous feedback for every move that takes the job posting in the desired direction.

Like all of the technologies we are examining, NLP is in early stages. As T continues to use data to drive its effectiveness evaluations, it learns to see a variety of cultural influences. The company's ultimate direction will be shaped by how well it learns to see into various companies and regional cultures. After all, communications effectiveness is a very localized sport.

Effective writing, guided to shape a specific outcome, is the heart of the textio service. In order to do that, the company must grasp an entire range of market dynamics. They're delivering real value while just touching the tip of the iceberg. Expect product extensions that deliver competitive insights, supply and demand, integration with other organizational functions and a broadening to other lines of communication.

ULTIMATE SOFTWARE (U)

When I asked whether they were making intelligence the heart of UtiliPro, U's chief data scientist, Moritz Sudhof, said, "No. Our culture is at the heart of everything." He did this earnestly, believably and without skipping a beat. It was one of the most astonishing moments in the process of creating this report.

U is and has been deeply committed to the notion that their tools are intended to enrich the lives of the people who use them. They want to improve cultural quality (effectiveness) in their client base by delivering functionality that fosters differentiation. They've gone as far as hiring a team of anthropologists.

They said:

> *"A delightful digital experience improves engagement and our new AI (named Xander™) & NLP engines process masses of structured/unstructured data instantly to provide rich actionable understanding of what is/isn't working. It provides deep specific insight and recommendations on cultural/managerial themes. Customers using the Xander-powered tool have an ongoing understanding of their employee's feelings about the workplace. They are 180% more successful than the S&P500, returning 54% vs. S&P's 18.8%."*

In September, 2016, U purchased Kanjoya, a sense-making startup that blended quantitative and qualitative data to grasp and synthesize employee feedback. The company has let the Kanjoya team go deep and build on existing data from U's nearly 25 years of history.

While we take other companies to task for loosely utilizing the term AI, U may be the real exception. Of course, there is no actual AI just yet. But, the company paints an astonishing picture of Xander's growing capabilities. The team with responsibility for Xander has the skill and resources required to defeat the obstacles between today's operation and a conversational interface that delivers situational insight.

It's the emphasis on the power of culture that sets them apart. It's hard to overstate how deeply U believes that harnessing employee communications can be used to completely transform, invigorate and optimize the performance of an organization.

A critical notion that is well developed at U is the idea of individual domain modeling. They believe that each HR silo has its own principles, puts, and takes. Then (almost paradoxically), they believe that cross domain data will be the ultimate keystone in their product development. The tool should be able to help nudge individual workflow streams into more positive directions.

The team goes to some lengths to say that Xander 'isn't going to replace anyone's job.' Meanwhile they are investing heavily in the physical infrastructure required to make Xander successful.

Ultimate combines ML, NLP, Sentiment Analysis and Quantitative survey tools to deliver its first intelligent product: Perception. This is one to watch.

WCN (W)
(World Careers Network plc)

W is a 20-year-old British public company traded on the London Exchange. Recent growth included expansion to the North American markets. In addition, they are expanding their offerings in a quest to become a full spectrum recruiting operation, which currently includes an ATS, Event Management module, Interview Scheduler and CRM. It's a long way from their roots as a college job board to their roadmap vision of Intelligent Talent Acquisition and they appear to be making great progress.

W makes great use of big data techniques to solve the problems of its primary clients. The combination of structured data and high-volume hiring make it possible to see patterns that would be harder in the absence of either or both conditions. The core claim is that W can tell you which of the 1000s of applications you receive from college graduates will result in interviews and hires for entry level jobs.

Over the course of its life, W built a deep and effective infrastructure. Long term stability leads to technical architectural infrastructure and employee optimization. The tech bench is deep, capable and understands the customer base.

One of the key initiatives at W involves maintaining ownership and control of their server and internet connection hardware. The decision involves one of the most difficult paradoxes in contemporary technical decision making.

While retaining ownership of bandwidth, storage and process is a great way to guarantee service reliability and provide high levels of security, it has the negative effect of limiting the company's access to the latest in predictive technologies. Processing, storage and bandwidth providers like Amazon and Google provide their clients with rapid access to the latest state of the art tools. The decision to go it alone is best understood as a tradeoff between customer experience and speed of innovation.

It is evidence that W puts customer experience first because they believe that technical change can be more effective at a slower pace. While much of the competition is aggressively chasing the next shiny object, W is making decisions at a slower pace.

That's the source of the dissonance in their messaging. On the one hand, the company makes coherent investment in the long-term success of their customers and has great relations with them. On the other, their marketing claims are much stronger than they need to be.

Structured data input systems like W, are fading from view. But, it's a slow fade. There is plenty of time to deploy the NLP tools that are broadly available to replace the legacy functionality. While it won't review as well, the company seems to have the sales muscle required to communicate the benefits of a tightly controlled process.

As long as there are volume hiring customers, W will be able to grow its market share. Features that reduce cycle time while improving the quality of the recruiting output are sorely needed. W is a demonstrated innovator in this slice.

WORKDAY (W)

Learning is never instantaneous. When an ML function has to absorb data from an entirely new situation, it takes a while to catch up. Leadership changes, Acquisitions, strategy shifts, disruptions, and, 'black swan' events all tax ML systems ability to predict. Every good ML system faces this challenge.

Three things differentiate W's approach:

1. Planning is a central utility function in the W stack. It is the only enterprise HR offering that weaves planning tools throughout. That means that natural disruptions (if there is such a thing) are more readily identified and managed.
2. The various elements of machine prediction and learning are embedded at a core level in the platform. The capacity s available for clients to deploy in unique ways. One of W's strengths is their devotion to the facilitation of customer innovation
3. The company emphasizes the combination of reduced time in the application and increased value.

While other platform players deliver some of these capabilities, only W delivers all three simultaneously.

As W considers the design and implementation of predictive tools the focus on timing (the moment insight is delivered matters), platform (the full integration of insight and data is critical), and context (the position of the ML output in the workflow). This design formula is intended to maximize the impact of any single bit of learned data that is returned to a user. Each interaction space is carefully architected.

W searches for business problems to solve. They see their foundational set of tools (Retention Analysis, Recommended Learning, Recruiting Search, Collections Analytics, Planning) as just that: the basis for future expansion.

When asked about what they've learned so far, W said some interesting things:

- ML is not just standalone. We have learned that it's not a unique app.
- ML is a toolkit
- Data and contextual data are the real source of value.
- This new tech demands a new way of thinking when developing products

This mindset, that predictive tools require a new way of thinking in software development is nascent among all of the enterprise level competitors. W is ahead of the game in its articulation of the new universe and the comprehensiveness of its vision.

Their strategy reflects this:
- Know the unknowns
- Do more with less
- Personalize experiences to make faster and better decisions.

Acknowledgments

Editing: Heather Bussing

Production: Anne Hill, JoJo Hill

Art: Ray Sumser

Conceptual Production: Stacey Harris, Holden Smith, Erin Spencer

I interviewed and debated with colleagues from all over the planet.

Jeanne Achille	China Gorman	Victorio Milian
Matt Alder	David Green	Kathy Missledine
George Anders	Kevin Grossman	Paul Mladineo
Anish Aravind	Chris Havrilla	Jeff Moore
Natalia Barishnakova	Mary Grace Hennessy	Cheryl Nelson
Meg Bear	Max Heywood	Stephen O'Donnell
Mark Bennett	D. Mark Hornung	Tim O'Shea
Kate Bischoff	Chris Hoyt	David Ossip
Steve Boese	Allen Johnson	Joy Capps Parrish
Mike Bollinger	Gareth Michael Jones	David Perry
Tom Bolt	John Jorgensen	Kent Plunkett
Ralph Brasker	Aki Kakko	Pete Radioff
Martin Burns	Michael Kannisto	Fran Rahl
Master Burnett	Andrew Karpie	Keith Robinson
Michael Carden	Peter Kazanjy	Lisa Rok
Rebecca Carr	Michael Kelleman	Peter Russell
Matt Charney	Katrina Kibben	Maureen Sharib
Mark Coleman	Bill Kutik	Luke Shipman
Mike Cooke	Kyle Lagunas	Brent Skinner
Bob Corlett	George LaRocque	Brian Sommer
Gerry Crispin	Madeline Tarquinio	Michael Specht
Alex Desjardins	Laurano	George Station
K.C. Donovan	Wendy Lawson	Mark Stelzner
David D'Souza	Jason Lauritsen	Lori Sylvia
Charlie Doucot	Hung Lee	Rayanne Thorn
Jonathan Duarte	Jessica Lee	Kristian Vanberg Jess
Bertrand Dussert	Jacob Sten Madsen	von Bank
Mary Faulkner	Oscar Mager	Brian Wempen
Andrew Gadomski	Marc Mapes	Felix Wetzel
Joe Gerstandt	Rob McIntosh	Brian Wis

About

ABOUT HREXAMINER

HRExaminer explores and researches the edges of HR, where Technology emerges and organizations transform. A research and publishing house, the company is known for the quality of its research and the prescience of its forecasts. The web magazine is fueled by a team of 25 'grey beard' writers who blend experience, curiosity, insight and a deep desire to continuously improve the industry. Visit hrexaminer.com .

ABOUT JOHN SUMSER

John is the founder and Principal Analyst at HRExaminer. He works diligently to make sure that HR professionals and leadership are aware of and prepared for the emerging technologies that shape HR. For 23 years, he has been helping shape the future with a plain-spoken, no nonsense approach to the intersection of HR and Technology.

CONTACT

Web: hrexaminer.com
Phone: 415.683.0775

John Sumser, *Principal Analyst*
@johnsumser
john@hrexaminer.com
+1.415.683.0775

Heather Bussing, *Principal Analyst*
@heatherbussing
heather@hrexaminer.com
+1.415.683.0775

Made in the USA
San Bernardino, CA
02 September 2018